The Queen of Hearts

A Pantomime

John Crocker

A Samuel French Acting Edition

Founded 1830

SAMUELFRENCH-LONDON.CO.UK
SAMUELFRENCH.COM

Copyright © 1967 by John Crocker and Eric Gilder
All Rights Reserved

THE QUEEN OF HEARTS is fully protected under the copyright laws of the British Commonwealth, including Canada, the United States of America, and all other countries of the Copyright Union. All rights, including professional and amateur stage productions, recitation, lecturing, public reading, motion picture, radio broadcasting, television and the rights of translation into foreign languages are strictly reserved.

ISBN 978-0-573-16438-5

www.samuelfrench-london.co.uk

www.samuelfrench.com

FOR AMATEUR PRODUCTION ENQUIRIES

UNITED KINGDOM AND WORLD EXCLUDING NORTH AMERICA

plays@SamuelFrench-London.co.uk

020 7255 4302/01

Each title is subject to availability from Samuel French, depending upon country of performance.

CAUTION: Professional and amateur producers are hereby warned that *THE QUEEN OF HEARTS* is subject to a licensing fee. Publication of this play does not imply availability for performance. Both amateurs and professionals considering a production are strongly advised to apply to the appropriate agent before starting rehearsals, advertising, or booking a theatre. A licensing fee must be paid whether the title is presented for charity or gain and whether or not admission is charged.

The professional rights in this play are controlled by Samuel French Ltd, 52 Fitzroy Street, London, W1T 5JR.

No one shall make any changes in this title for the purpose of production. No part of this book may be reproduced, stored in a retrieval system, or transmitted in any form, by any means, now known or yet to be invented, including mechanical, electronic, photocopying, recording, videotaping, or otherwise, without the prior written permission of the publisher. No one shall upload this title, or part of this title, to any social media websites.

The right of John Crocker to be identified as author of this work has been asserted by him in accordance with Section 77 of the Copyright, Designs and Patents Act 1988

PRODUCTION NOTE

Pantomime, as we know it today, is a form of entertainment all on its own, derived from a number of different sources - the commedia dell'arte (and all that derived from), the ballet, the opera, the music hall and the realms of folk-lore and fairy tale. And elements of all of these are still to be found in it. This strange mixture has created a splendid topsy-turvy world where men are women, women are men, where the present is embraced within the past, where people are hit but not hurt, where authority is constantly flouted, where fun is poked at everything including pantomime itself at times and, above all, where magic abounds and dreams invariable come true. In other words, it is - or should be - fun. Fun to do and fun to watch and the sense of enjoyment which can be conveyed by a cast is very important to the enjoyment of the audience.

Pantomime can be very simply staged if resources are limited. Basically a tab surround at the back, tab legs at the sides and a set of traverse tabs for the frontcloth scenes, together with the simplest of small cut-out pieces to suggest the various locales, (or even just placards with this information written on them), will suffice. Conversely, there is no limit to the extent to which more lavish facilities can be employed. If the effects in Scene 5 are too difficult to achieve as indicated, then the ballet should be modified to avoid them.

The directions I have given in the text adopt a middle course and are based on a permanent setting of a cyclorama sky-cloth at the back, a few feet in front of which is a rostrum about two feet high, running the width of the stage. About two thirds of the depth downstage is a false proscenium, immediately behind which are the lines for a set of traverse tabs. Below the false proscenium are arched entrances left and right, with possible one foot reveals to the proscenium. A border will be necessary at some point between the false proscenium and the cyclorama to mask lighting battens and the top of the cyclorama. Lastly, there is a set of steps leading from the front of the stage into the auditorium, which I have referred to as the catwalk. I have imagined it to be set stage left, but it is unimportant whether it is left or right.

Into this permanent setting are placed various wings left and right, (I have catered for one a side set on a level with the border, but a greater depth of stage may require two a side for masking purposes). Cut-out ground-rows set on the front or back of the rostrum complete the full sets. On smaller stages these cut-outs seen against the cyclorama give a better impression of depth than backcloths. The frontcloth fly lines come in behind the traverse tabs. Cloths can, of course, be tumbled or rolled if flying space is limited. It is a good tip always to bring in the traverse tabs when a cloth has to be lowered, then if any hitch occurs the lights can still come up and the actors get on with the scene. Similarly, I have indicated where the traverse tabs should be closed in frontcloth scenes so that there is plenty of time for the cloth to be flown before the end of the scene. The quick flow of one scene into the next is important if a smooth running production is to be achieved.

The settings should preferably be in clear bright colours to give a story book effect. The main costumes of the King, Queen and Knave should be as like those in a pack of cards as possible and it is, of course, preferable to try to have a similar style for the other characters, although deliberate anachronisms can be introduced into some of the comic's costumes and some of the settings. It is important for Scene 8 that there should be easily recognisable differences in the Sorcerers's costumes so that when the others are disguised as them there is no doubt as to who is impersonating who. The Moon Monster's costume can be made of hessian painted or dyed, with a strip of tartan about nine inches wide at the bottom for the kilt. The hessian is shaped to form the humps into which the Chorus put their heads and there should be gauze eyepieces let into the front of each hump. The front should fit over the shoulders of the principal with two armholes for him to get his forearms through. These should be covered by separate gloved sleeves. The headpiece - rather shaggy and dragon-like - should also be separate and it should allow his face, suitably made-up, to be clearly seen. The principal and the Chorus should wear identical trousers to represent scaly legs. There should be armholes by number 3 legs to operate the wings.
Bomzo's skin can be hired from Theatre Zoo, London.

Pantomime requires many props and often they will have to be home made. Instructions are given in the prop plot about any of the more awkward seeming ones. Props should also be colourfully painted and in pantomime most props should be much larger than reality. It is also wise for the property master to examine carefully the practical use to which a prop is to be put - it is very painful to be hit with a 'Bumper Biffer' club of solid wood, one of material filled with foam plastic is far gentler!

I have not attempted to give a lighting plot as this entirely depends on the equipment available, but, generally speaking, most pantomime lighting needs to be full up, warm and bright. Pinks and ambers are probably best for this, but a circuit of blues in the cyclorama battens would be useful for the Moon scene.

Follow spots are a great help for this kind of show, but not essential. If they are available it is often effective in romantic numbers to fade out the stage lighting and hold the principals in the follow spots, quickly fading up on the last few bars because this can help to increase the applause! They can also be used for the Fairy and Demon to give them greater freedom of movement than with fixed front of house or spot-bar spots.

Flash boxes with the necessary colour and flash powders and maroons can be obtained from the usual stage electrical suppliers.

The music has been specially composed so that it is easy for the less musically accomplished to master, but it is also scored in parts for the more ambitious. If an orchestra is available well and good, but a single piano will suffice. It is an advantage, however, if there can be a drummer as well. Not only because a rhythm accompaniment enhances the numbers, but also because for some reason never yet fully fathomed slapstick hits and falls are always twice as funny if they coincide with a well-timed bonk on a drum, wood-block or whatever is found to make the noise best suited to the action. A drummer can also cope with the "Tings" and "Whizzes" noted in the directions, though, of course, they can if necessary be done offstage. A special type of whistle can be got for the "Whizz" and the "Ting" requires a triangle.

Pantomime demands a particular style of playing and production. The acting must be larger than life, but still sincere, with a good deal of sparkle and attack. Much of it must be projected directly at the audience, since one of pantomime's great advantages is that is deliberately breaks down the "fourth wall". The actors can literally and metaphorically shake hands with their audience who become almost another member of the cast; indeed, their active participation from time to time is essential. A word of warning, though, on this - the actors must always remain in control; for instance, if a Demon or villain encourages hissing he must make sure it is never to such an extent that he can no longer be heard. The producer should see that the story line is clearly brought out and treated with respect. This is particularly important in this pantomime where there is no well-known story, but one that I have elaborated from the few details of the nursery rhyme, which as it will be fresh to the audience will have to be put over to them with especial care. There is always room for local gags and topical quips in pantomime, but they should not be overdone. Most important of all, the comedy, as any comedy, must never appear to be conscious of its own funniness.

Characterization should be very clear and definite. I prefer the traditional use of a man to play the Dame and a girl to play the Principal Boy. In the case of the Dame, anyway, there is a sound argument for this - audiences will laugh more readily at a man impersonating a women involved in the mock cruelties of slapstick than a real woman. For this reason an actor playing a Dame should never quite let us forget he is a man, while giving a sincere character performance of a woman; further, he can be as feminine as he likes, but never effeminate. The Queen is boisterous and essentially an optimist. Though clearly the dominant partner she should never appear to despise or hen-peck her spouse. They should have a sincere affection for each other for the King is by no means a fool. Paradoxically, although he is almost speechless, it can be a very telling part. To be so it must be played with great concentration, as this is perhaps more essential in a mime part than any other. To gain the full effect when he does speak in Scene 10, it is important that he should not utter a word until then. The actor must be wary not to be trapped into any gagging earlier.

Like the Dame, a Principal Boy also requires a character performance, but, of course, with the implications reversed! An occasional slap of the thigh is not sufficient. The Prince should be thought of as a very charming light comedian and played with a sense of fun and a light touch.

Principal Girls can be a bore, but only if they are presented as mere pretty symbols of feminine sweetness. The Princess is lively and very human. She is laughter-loving, but not frivolous, for she has a decided mind of her own and intends to use it.

The Ace has a deep sense of duty towards his villainy. Unfortunately he is far less successful at it than he would like to imagine. Perhaps because, although he does not realise it, his is fundamentally a kind and courteous nature. In these qualities his son Jack, the Knave, emulates him, but he is fully aware of his limitations as a villain. Any efforts he makes to improve himself in this respect are purely out of family loyalty. He is not really a fool, but just one of those people who always seem to find themselves holding the wrong end of the stick. His beloved, W.P.C. Penny, is very eager - one imagines she was jolly good at hockey at school - but it is an engaging eagerness. Her dog, Bonzo, is lumbering, bumbling and slow-witted but also very lovable.

The Sorcerers live in a world of their own. It is not an idiotic world, just different from anyone else's. Perhaps it is a better one, because inspite of their advanced age, both are very sprightly.

Rummy is a highly supercilious fellow. If desired he can be doubled with the Moon Monster, who, though fearsome looking, is a she, retiring, rather endearing creature.

The Fairy Patience is a staunch country lass. While not smug, she is fully convinced of the rightness of her point of view. The Racing Demon Snap is likewise equally convinced of his - opposing - point of view, but he is rather cocky about it. He is younger than most Demons and should be played as very modern and brash.

I have made provision for six members of the Chorus, but naturally the number used will depend on how many are available.

John Crocker.

CHARACTERS

THE PRINCESS OF HEARTS

W. P. C. PENNY

THE LORD HIGH ACE OF HEARTS

JACK, THE KNAVE OF HEARTS — His Son

BONZO — A Bloodhound

THE PRINCE OF DIAMONDS

THE KING OF HEARTS

THE QUEEN OF HEARTS

RUMMY — A Footman

MERLIN — The Court Sorcerer

MERLOUT — His Apprentice

THE FAIRY PATIENCE

THE RACING DEMON SNAP

THE MOON MONSTER

CHORUS as Inhabitants of Heartland, Fairies, Imps, Court Ladies, six-sevenths of Monster, etc.

SYNOPSIS OF SCENES

PART I

SCENE 1. THE LAND OF HEARTS.

SCENE 2. A FATEFUL MEETING.

SCENE 3. THE ROYAL KITCHEN.

SCENE 4. THE PALACE PORTRAIT GALLERY.

SCENE 5. A CROWDED CORNER OF FAIRYLAND.

SCENE 6.	THE ROYAL BANQUET.
SCENE 7.	ON THE WAY TO THE DEN.
SCENE 8.	THE SORCERERS' DEN.
SCENE 9.	IN THE AIR.
SCENE 10.	ON THE MOON.
SCENE 11.	DOWN TO EARTH.
SCENE 12.	THE GRAND WEDDING RECEPTION AT THE HOUSE OF CARDS.

- - - - - - - - - - - - - - - - -

Running Time approximately 2 hours 35 minutes.

MUSIC 1. Overture

ACT ONE

Scene One - THE LAND OF HEARTS

(Full set. Cut-out ground row along back of rostrum showing distant view of palace. Palace gates in C. front of rostrum. Steps down in front of them. Wing piece R. "YE OLDE ROYAL FLUSH". Wing piece L. "YE NEWE SORCERERS DEN" with practical door. Trick doormat in front of it. Painted window U.S. of door with window box attached in front of it. Flowers on lines to "grow" out of it concealed inside it. In front of pros arch R., a small cut-out well without bucket or rope.

CHORUS discovered as inhabitants of Heartland singing and dancing opening Chorus. During number one of Chorus waters window box with watering can and flowers "grow".)

(MUSIC 2. "It's Summer")

CHORUS: It's Summer,
The first day of Summer.
When today the sun began to rise
And we rubbed the sleep out of our eyes,
Then we said we'd sing a song to welcome
The sweet newcomer.
Good morning.
Good heavens!
Good weather!!
Now the birds can really start to sing
That we've seen the last this year of Spring -
It's Summer, it's Summer, it's Summer!

PENNY: (off R.) Police parade, quick march!

(MUSIC 3. Enter PENNY marching.)

CHORUS: Good morning, P.C. Penny.

PENNY: (marking time) Ssh, not at the moment. I'm on my inspection parade.

1st CH: Who are you going to inspect?

PENNY: Me, of course, I'm all the police there are to inspect, except my faithful bloodhound, Bonzo. Police halt! (She halts.) Police, right turn! (She turns L.) Police, you're an idiot. About turn! (She about turns to face Audience.) One, inspect whistle. (Takes out her whistle and blows it, no sound comes.)

(CHORUS laugh.)

Well, I took the pea out. It was so awfully noisy. Two, inspect truncheon. (Brings out a large dog bone.)

(CHORUS laugh.)

Oh, really! That's Bonzo's fault. He's such a fool, that dog. I suppose he's buried my truncheon somewhere. Three, inspect siren on police scooter. The scooter! Where is it? I've been robbed! Help, police!

(CHORUS laugh.)

Oh, that's me, isn't it? Ooh, goody I'll be able to make my first arrest. How super! I'll summon myself at once. (Blows whistle.) That's no good, I can't hear it. I'll get Bonzo to track them down. Bonzo! Bonzo!

(EFFECT 1. Sound of police siren off L.)

2nd CH: Listen! This must be the thief now!

3rd CH: (looking off L.) It isn't. It's the Princess!

(MUSIC 4. Enter PRINCESS on police scooter L. She circles round on it.)

PRINCESS: Whee!

CHORUS: Your highness.

PRINCESS: (tries to wave regally to them) Oops, sorry, I can't give you my royal wave on this. It's too wobbly.

4th CH: P.C. Penny will be glad you've found it.

PRINCESS: Found it? Nonsense, I've stolen it! Whee! (She scoots to R. almost running into PENNY as she enters there.)

PENNY: (curtseying) Oh, your high - My scooter!

PRINCESS: Dear me, caught red-handed.

PENNY: You've found - caught did you say?

PRINCESS: Yes, Penny, I cannot tell a lie. At least, not when I can't get away with it. I stole your scooter. (Gives it to PENNY.)

PENNY: Oh, what a disappointment. I'm not allowed to arrest Royalty.

PRINCESS: What a nuisance it is to be priviliged. All the exciting things aren't allowed to happen to one.

1 - 1 - 3

PENNY: What about the banquet tonight to celebrate your betrothal to the Prince of Diamonds? I should have thought that was pretty exciting.

PRINCESS: Hardly. We've been sort of betrothed all our lives. Tonight's do is just to make it official. The only snag is, we've never met, and we shan't until the banquet. Well, it's a bit late then if we hate the sight of each other, isn't it?

PENNY: There now, if you were me you could get a peek at him this morning. I'm putting myself on special security duty for his arrival.

PRINCESS: What a splendid idea, Penny. I will be you.

PENNY: Yes, rather - eh?

PRINCESS: I'll be you.

PENNY: But how?

PRINCESS: (urging her to R.) In one of your uniforms, of course. You'd better look it out now.

PENNY: But, your highness -

PRINCESS: No more "buts", Penny. Off you go.

PENNY: But there's something - vital!

PRINCESS: Vital?

(PENNY whispers in here ear.)

PRINCESS: Oh, vital. 36-24-34. (Or whatever PRINCESS feels flatters her most.)

PENNY: (looks at her own figure) Well, I daresay it will be somewhe: or other. (She runs off R. on scooter.)

PRINCESS: I think our police are marvellous.

(CHORUS laugh.)

I wish I could feel the same about my future husband.

5th CH: Cheer up, your highness. I've heard he's very handsome.

6th CH: And awfully rich.

PRINCESS: But is he gay? Is he kind? Is he strong? Is he gentle? Most of all, is he a man I can love?

(MUSIC 5. "The Man for me".)

Is he tall? Is he smart?
Has he flair? Has he heart?
   Just how old is his family tree?
Has he nerve? Has he taste?
Does he bow from the waist?
   Who is the man for me?

Is he bass? Does he squeak?
Does he bath every week?
   Is he known in Society?
Is he dry? Is he wet?
Is he Mum's little pet?
   Who is the man for me?

Is he open and frank or is he mystic?
   The sepculation keeps me pretty busy.
He may say that he's wealthy and artistic,
   But the question that I ask myself is "Is he?"

Is he this? Is he that?
Is it love, or just chat?
   Is he loaded with L.S.D. ?
Is he dark? Is he fair?
Has he curls? Has he hair!'.!
   Who is the man for me?

Is he brave, or a mouse?
Is he clean in the house?
   Is he good at Monopoly?
Does he sniff, does he snore,
Drop his ash on the floor?
   Who is the man for me?

Is he kind to his folks?
Does he laugh at his jokes?
   Does he watch only ITV?
Is he all skin and bone?
Does he weigh twenty stone?
   Who is the man for me?

When I think of the likely permutations,
   The situation puts me in a tizzy.
Is his blood like a new United Nations?
   Is he Fred or Pat or Mac or is he Issie?

>   Never mind, never mind.
>   If he's good and he's kind
>   And he holds me with sympathy,
>   If there's love in his heart,
>   Then I'll know from the start,
>   That is the man for me.

(Exit PRINCESS R. and CHORUS variously.)

ACE: (off L.) Make way for me! Make way for me!

(MUSIC 6. Enter ACE L.)

Make way for - Curses! Nobody here to make way for me - me, the chief officer of state, the Lord High Ace of Hearts himself and I'm ignored. I wouldn't mind if I was thoroughly disliked - unpopularity is the burden of the dedicated villain like myself - but to be ignored. I wonder, would you do something for me? Would you indulge me by saying "Hiss-Boo!" whenever I appear? You would? Good. Let's try it. "Hiss-Boo!" (Cups hand to ear.) Not bad, but a little louder - "HISS-BOO!" (Cups hand to ear again.) Splendid! But only say it once each time, I'm not bad enough for more. We'll have one last try. I'll go off this time and you shout out as soon as you see me look on and say "Aha!" (Exit L.) Stand by. (MUSIC 7. Puts head on.) "Aha!" (Audience shout. He re-enters.) Ah, most reassuring. Now I shan't feel ignored. I couldn't bear to be a failure as a villain. I'm afraid my son Jack, the Knave of Hearts, is a failure though. He doesn't even like villainy. But I shall persevere with him. I owe it to the memory of his poor dear mother - ah, what a lovely villainess she was. A real lady - killer. Why, she even took the trouble to lace my tea with arsenic. What a pity the day she put a treble dose in she forgot and drank it herself. Yes, for her sake I'll make a decent blackguard of Jack yet.

JACK: (off L.) Hic! Hic!

ACE: Whatever's that?

JACK: (off) Hic! Hic!

ACE: Some country bumpkin or "Hick", no doubt. He-he-he! What a piercing wit I have. (Looks off L.) Good heavens! It's Jack!

(MUSIC 8. Enter JACK L. carrying a huge club projecting from the pages of a magazine.)

JACK: Father! - Hic! - Father'.

ACE: What's the matter, Jack?

JACK: Matter? Noth-hic-ing.

ACE: Yes, there is. You've got hiccups.

JACK: Oh, hic! have I? Well, I always do when I'm hic - cited and I don't no - hic - tice.

ACE: Well, now you have noticed do something to stop it.

JACK: Well, you give me a shock when I'm not hic - specting it. Say hic - boo.

ACE: Say hic - boo?

JACK: No, just hic - I mean, boo. When I'm not hic - specting it. I'm not hic - specting it now. Hic.

ACE: Very well. Boo.

JACK: There you see, cured it. Hic! Almost.

ACE: I know how to give you a real shock. Just stay there while I go away and come back again.

JACK: Eh? Hic!

ACE: (aside to AUDIENCE) Very loud. (Exit R. MUSIC 9. Pokes head on.) Aha!

(AUDIENCE shout. JACK jumps. ACE re-enters.)

JACK: Ooh, that's stopped it. But why did they do that?

ACE: A little private arrangement I have with them. Now, what were you excited about?

JACK: I've done my good deed for the day.

ACE: What! How dare you break a cad's honour like that. You're supposed to do a dirty deed every day. I keep telling you, now I've had you created the official Knave of Hearts you must be more knavish. What was this horrible good deed you did?

JACK: I went to the newsagents and got your this week's "Scoundrel".

ACE: Oh, well that was very thoughtful of you, my boy. (Takes it.) Let's see. Ooh, "Given free with this week's issue of "Scoundrel", a Bumper Biffer. Well, where is it? (Turns pages until club is full revealed.) Ah, just what I've always wanted. We can put it to use right away. Hist! I'm going to hatch a plot.

JACK: I thought you looked broody.

ACE: Tcha! Will you kindly learn to take villainy seriously. Now, as you know, for a number of years I have been embezzling the country's taxes. The money thus obtained I have lent to the King and Queen. A nice touch that, I thought, lending them their own money unbeknownst to themselves, eh? He-he-he-he. (Digs KNAVE in ribs.) Well, laugh, boy.

JACK: (hollowly) Ha-ha-ha-ha. (Digs ACE in ribs a little forcibly.)

ACE: Ouch! Don't overdo it. Now, this money they have agreed to repay by tomorrow, because they think that by then they will have sealed the betrothal of their daughter to the Prince of Diamonds. And, on his son's behalf, the King of Diamonds has promised a handsome gift for the Princess's hand.

JACK: Only for her hand? What about the rest of her?

ACE: He's promised an even more handsome gift. But listen carefully because it gets very involved here. If something happens to stop the match and they can't repay their debt to me, then I can force them to abdicate and rule the kingdom - through you.

JACK: Through me? How?

ACE: I'll come to that bit in a minute. Something _will_ happen to stop the match.

JACK: What?

ACE: (as if it explained everything) No jam tarts!

JACK: Ah! Eh?

ACE: No jam tarts. Think, lad. Surely you, like everybody else, know that in the Land of Hearts a royal betrothal must be sealed by the happy couple eating jam tarts made by the Queen's own hand.

JACK: Oh, _that._ Yes, well, I knew that, of course.

ACE: Of course. Well, the King and Queen have just enough money to buy the ingredients for some tarts. So this morning they'll be sending their footman, Rummy, on a little shopping expedition. But - if someone waylays him and steals the ingredients they've no more money, so no jam tarts - no tarts, no betrothal - no betrothal, no handsome gifts, - no handsome gifts, no repayment - no repayment, I take over the kingdom and rule - through you.

JACK: Why through me?

1 - 1 - 8

ACE: Because as the match with the Prince of Diamonds will be off you are going to marry the Princess and become King Jack the First. Well, to work. You will doubtless have guessed now how we, or rather you, can use this Bumper Biffer. (Hands it to JACK.)

JACK: Er - no.

ACE: Tut-tut, I should have thought it was clear enough. You biff Rummy, of course, and steal the ingredients for the tarts. I'm sure I can rely on you to make a good job of it.

JACK: I'm not. How do you use it?

ACE: You just swing it and biff with the big end.

JACK: Swing it? Like this? (Takes a sideways swipe and spins round with the weight of it inadvertently knocking ACE on arm and tumbling him over.)

ACE: Ow! No, not like that.

JACK: Sorry. Like this then? (Just as ACE is rising he swings it back over his head, knocking ACE on behind with the upswing and staggering back.)

Oops. (Swings it forward over head even more out of control and hits ACE on head. ACE subsides.) Yes, I think I'm getting the hang of it, father. (Looks down at ACE's prostrate form.) Father! Oh dear. Hic! Father, speak to me, father! Hic!

ACE: Where am I?

JACK: Sitting on the floor. Was that right? Hic.

ACE: Right! Hic! (Rubbing head.) You've cracked my skull -

BOTH: Hic!

ACE: (rising, rubbing bottom) Dislocated my -

BOTH: Hic!

ACE: And further more given me your -

BOTH: Hic!

ACE: Cups. I shall retire to the Royal Flush for running repairs. Hic! And you'd better leave Rummy to me. I don't want you bungling that. Hic! (Exit R.)

JACK: Yes, father. Hic! Oh, he'll want this, then. Here, father! (Throws Biffer R. as ACE re-enters so that it hits him in stomach.)

1 - 1 - 9

ACE: OW! Now, look what you've done.

JACK: Sorry. Still, it's cured your hiccups.

ACE: Cured my - ! Doh! (Exit R.)

JACK: Cured mine too. I'm afraid I'm a great disappointment to father. Especially since I came back from university without a degree in Felony. Well, I was all right on the theory, but they failed me on the practical - I didn't try to steal the answers. Poor father, he did so want me to be a Bachelor of Felony, so that he could say I was a B. F. Well, all the rest of the family are, you see.

PENNY: (off R.) Bonzo! Bonzo!

BONZO: (off R.) Wuff! Wuff!

(MUSIC 10. BONZO runs on R. with a truncheon in his mouth. PENNY chases on after him.)

PENNY: Bonzo, give me back my truncheon at once!

(BONZO runs below KNAVE and U.S. in a wide circle. PENNY follows and stops as she comes abreast of KNAVE. BONZO stops to note this.)

Pardon me, sir. (Salutes.)

JACK: Eh? Oh, me, yes. (Raises hat.)

(BONZO and PENNY start running again. BONZO circles D.S to run past KNAVE. PENNY stops momentarily as she comes abreast of JACK again and salutes. JACK raises his hat. BONZO stops to note PENNY and then both run off D.L.)

Perhaps it's the police sports.

(BONZO runs on above L. wing and to below JACK stopping as he comes abreast of him.)

BONZO: (saluting) Wuff!

JACK: Er - wuff. (Raises hat.)

(BONZO runs off D.R. as PENNY runs on above L. wing and comes to below JACK, who raises hat preparatory to being saluted, but she runs past him without stopping.)

JACK: (replacing hat) Pity. I wish she'd stayed long enough for me to meet her.

1 - 1 - 10

(PENNY dashes on anove R. wing and pulls up sharply as she realises BONZO is not ahead of her)

PENNY: Oh. (Shoots look up and down stage.)

JACK: I say -

(PENNY salutes, turns and dashes off above wing again, leaving KNAVE raising hat to her. BONZO saunters on D.R. JACK bends to talk with him with legs astride)

JACK: Hullo. I think someone's after you.

BONZO: (nods happily)

(PENNY backs on D.R.)

PENNY: Oh, Bonzo, where are - (Turns.) Bonzo! (As she moves down to grab him, BONZO streaks through JACK'S legs. PENNY moves forward on all fours and is about to go through also, then stops.) May I?

JACK: Oh, certainly.

PENNY: Thanks. (Crawls forward and stops between his legs) Oh. (Salutes.)

(JACK raises hat. BONZO re-enters D.L. without truncheon. PENNY rises toppling JACK over.)

PENNY: Bonzo! Oh, sorry, sir. (Salutes.)

JACK: (raising hat) Not at all. (Rises.)

PENNY: Bonzo, where is it? You haven't buried it, have you?

BONZO (looks sheepish)

PENNY: Oh, Bonzo. That wasn't a bone, it was my truncheon, dear.

BONZO: (looks astounded)

PENNY: Go and dig it up, Bonzo.

BONZO: (goes disconsolately off L.)

PENNY: Sorry, about all that, sir. I'm afraid Bonzo's not very bright. (BONZO enters L. dejectedly and gives PENNY truncheon) That's a good boy. Now sit, dear.

BONZO: (begs)

PENNY: No, sit.

BONZO: (nods)

PENNY: Oh, all right then, beg.

BONZO: (sits)

PENNY: You see, misunderstands every word I say. By the way, I hope you don't mind me talking to you like this.

JACK: Mind?

PENNY: Well, you are the Knave and all that. You might think it's the most awful cheek.

JACK: Oh no, I think it's rather nice. In fact, I think you're rather - hic! hic!

PENNY: I say, you've got hiccups.

JACK: Hic! Have I?

PENNY: Yes. Water's what you need. Where can we find water, Bonzo?

BONZO: (puts a forepaw to head to think. A brilliant idea strikes him and he bounds off L.)

PENNY: Goodness, surely he didn't know what I meant.

(BONZO re-enters with a divining rod)

He did! Clever, Bonzo.

JACK: Yes - hic! and what a devine rod.

BONZO: (divines round stage. Rod starts to get very active as he comes C. He points to C. of floats)

PENNY: He's found some!

BONZO: (gives rod to PENNY and "digs" in floats with his forepaws)

PENNY: Is it a hidden spring, Bonzo?

BONZO: (nods) Wuff! (Proudly brings up a large bed spring.)

PENNY: (taking it) Oh no, Bonzo, not this kind of spring. (throws it off.) Isn't there anything else?

BONZO: (sniffs at "hole", nods and digs again)

PENNY: What is it?

BONZO: (happily brings up a large bone and exits L. with it)

PENNY: Oh, Bonzo.

JACK: Never mind. Hic.

PENNY: But we must find some water to stop your hiccups.

JACK: Perhaps there's some in this old well. Hic. (Takes divining rod to well by pros. arch. Rod waggles vigorously.) There is! Hic. But there's no rope or bucket to get it out.

PENNY: May be it's a wishing well. Try a wish.

JACK: All right. Hic. I wish for some water. (Water squirts up into his face.) Not like that, hic! In a glass, some hiccup water.

(MUSIC 11. A glass of water with straws rises on a line from well)

Ooh. (Drinks.) Ta.

(MUSIC 12. Glass goes down)

It's cured them. It's very good hiccup water.

(MUSIC 13. Glass rises)

No, I'm all right now.

(MUSIC 14. Glass goes down)

PENNY: I say, perhaps it always comes up when you say hiccup water.

(MUSIC 15. Glass rises)

JACK: Ooh yes. That's given me an idea. (To glass.) All right thanks.

(MUSIC 16. Glass goes down)

(to AUDIENCE) Would you help me? You see, I don't notice when I get hiccups, so would you notice for me? Whenever I start hiccuping you shout "Hiccup water!"

(MUSIC 17. Glass rises)

Would you do that? Oh, thank you. Let's try it. (Sees glass.) Down again, please.

(MUSIC 18. Glass goes down)

Right, I'll hiccup and you shout "Hiccup water! Hic! Hic!

(AUDIENCE shout. MUSIC 19. Glass comes up a little way and than goes down.)

I think you'll have to shout a bit louder. Once more. Hic! Hic!

(AUDIENCE shout. MUSIC 20. Glass shoots up.)

That's more like it. (To glass.) Thank you. Sorry to overwork you.

(MUSIC 21. Glass goes down.)

They shout jolly well, don't they?

PENNY: Oh, absolutely super. But why don't you notice your hiccups?

JACK: 'Cos I only get them when I'm excited. You see, I'd just met you and you were rather - rather - hic! Hic!

(AUDIENCE shout. MUSIC 22. Glass rises. JACK rushes and takes drink.)

Thanks.

(MUSIC 23. Glass goes down.)

PENNY: Did you really think I was rather - hic?

(JACK nods shyly)

That's the nicest thing anybody's ever said to me. Oh, I feel as happy as if I'd arrested somebody.

JACK: Well, I wish you'd arrest me. I'd do anything for you - forge a cheque, rob a bank, even park on a yellow line.

PENNY: Would you? Then it looks as if I'll have to take you in charge, doesn't it?

(MUSIC 24. "The Copping Song")

JACK:
   I'm a rotten rotter;
   I do wrong because I gotter,
   And I lead a life of wickedness and sin.
   I'm a shocking crook
   And I should go down in your book
   As just the sort of chap you should be running in.

PENNY: (writing) At 9.15 on the 27th,
   As I was on my beat,
   I was accosted by a man -
   And the things he said were sweet!

1 - 1 - 14

JACK: I'm an awful bounder,
A felonious all-rounder;
Don't you think you should consider an arrest?
That's a thing to brag on,
If you'd take me in your wagon.
Won't you please do your constabulary best?

PENNY: I understand that he was asking
Me to be his wife.

BOTH: I/He wouldn't ask for more
Than the arms of the law
For Life!

(DANCE)

PENNY: (writing) So I decided to uphold
the dignity of the Force.

JACK: You needn't tell the Sarge.
Are you taking me in charge?

PENNY: Of course! (They kiss.)

(they exit. MUSIC 25. ACE pokes head on R.)

ACE: Aha!

(AUDIENCE shout. ACE enters.)

Ah, splendid. Some of the best "boos" I've ever had. Well having fortified the inner man, now I must attend to my injuries.

QUEEN: (off R.) Keep going, Oswald!

ACE: (looks off R.) Their Majesties! If I'm not careful, Rummy will be back with the shopping before I am. I must hurry and hold up a hospital for some free first aid. (He hobbles off L.)

(MUSIC 26. Enter KING and QUEEN OF HEARTS R. carrying a sedan chair on side of which is a curtained window and a royal coat of arms painted below it. The QUEEN is at the front and has a cloak which trails behind her.)

QUEEN: (stopping in C.) Whew! I do wish we didn't have such heavy appearances to keep up, Oswald.

(they lower sedan, QUEEN onto the end of her cloak, KING apparently onto his U.S. foot)

KING: Ow!

QUEEN: (running forward) What's the - (She is brought up short and pulled over onto her back by her trapped cloak.) Oh, really! You know, life was much easier when we were able to afford a staff to carry us in this thing. Especially as we have to carry the staff now. Rummy!... Rummy!!

RUMMY: (draws curtains and pokes head out of window) You called, your Majesty?

QUEEN: Yes, Rummy.

RUMMY: Something important I trust, your Majesty, I was just dozing off.

QUEEN: Well, if it wouldn't be too inconvenient, Rummy, I require a little help.

RUMMY: (sighs) Very well, your Majesty. (He opens door at front of sedan and moves out head held superciliously high, so that he does not see QUEEN.) Where is your Majesty? (Stops with a foot planted on her.)

QUEEN: Under your dirty great -

RUMMY: (looking down) Oh, I see. Under my right pedal extremity.

QUEEN: You took the very words out of my mouth. Well, perhaps you'd remove it and help me to my pedal - whatever-you-said.

RUMMY: (sighs) I'll try, your Majesty. (Removes foot and tilts front of sedan up hitting KING on head with the back of it as he is bent forward rubbing his foot.) Oops, beg your other Majesty's pardon. (Clears train from under sedan and moves to help QUEEN up) Ups a royal daisy.

QUEEN: That's better. Are you all right, Oswald?

(KING moves down limping, rubbing head and groaning)

QUEEN: Ah, good. Now, Rummy, you can go and buy the things I need to make the special jam tarts for tonight's banquet. Some flour, butter jam and salt.

RUMMY: Yes, your Majesty. Only - what with, if you'll pardon such a vulgar question?

(KING opens mouth)

QUEEN: Oswald! No vulgar answers, please. Unfortunately I'm not sure of a polite one. Unless - Oswald, just look and see if our Sorcerers have discovered how to turn lead into gold yet.

(KING moves to SORCERER'S Den L., the door of which opens in his face. MUSIC 27. Enter MERLOUT with a dustbin labelled 'FAILED EXPERIMENTS" and places it on trick doormat by door. KING shuts door rubbing his nose and it is immediately opened in his face again by MERLIN carrying a mess labelled "EXPERIMENT 904". KING shuts door.

MERLIN: You forgot one.

(MERLOUT lifts lid and MERLIN tips it into dustbin.)

Right, let's get started on nine hundred and five.

(KING dodges head aside as door is opened and SORCERERS exit, but is caught again by it as MERLIN returns, takes out a small wand and waves it over dustbin which is pulled off on trick cloth. MERLIN exits.

QUEEN: Well, that seems to settle that point. There's only one thing for it, Oswald - the Royal Exchequer.

(KING looks puzzled)

QUEEN: Yes, dear, you know, the piggy bank.

KING: (brings out a small piggy bank)

QUEEN: (taking it) Thank you, Oswald. (Opens it.) Dear me, the Royal Exchequer's rather low. (takes out a coin.) In fact, this is it. Rummy, you must be very careful with the shopping. It's essential that I make those tarts and there's nothing to buy any more ingredients.

RUMMY: Very well, your Majesty. But the shops are several yards down the road. How am I to get there?

QUEEN: I suggest you bicycle.

RUMMY: Bicycle?

QUEEN: Yes, on your pedal extremities.

(RUMMY moves L. mumbling to himself. He drops coin and as he bends to pick it up reveals a large heart embroidered on his costume over his behind.

QUEEN: Dear Rummy. He's a bit touchy, but his hearts in the right place.

(exit Rummy L.)

I say, it's very deserted today, isn't it, Oswald?

(KING opens mouth to speak)

I knew you'd agree. Well, you always do, don't you?

(KING shakes head)

QUEEN: What's that, Oswald?

(KING hurriedly nods head)

Silly me, I must have misheard you. Yes, very deserted. Where's the usual vast crowd to welcome us?

(KING points to AUDIENCE)

There? (Moves to peer at AUDIENCE.) Oh, yes, a vast crowd indeed. Rather difficult to take a royal butchers at them in all this dark, though. You don't happen to have a torch with you?

(KING nods and takes out a small torch.)

Ah, dear Oswald - ever ready. But it's a bit small. We'll have to pick them out one by one.

(KING shakes head and spreads arms to indicate all the AUDIENCE.)

Oh, not with that surely, Oswald?

(KING nods.)

Well, switch it on and let's see.

(KING switches it on. HOUSELIGHTS UP.)

Goodness, what a powerful beam. Do you think you should make a speech, dear?

(KING nods and clears throat.)

Yes, as the King and Queen of Hearts we welcome you to our land. Right, that's enough, Oswald. He does ramble on so, you know. Ah, I see our royal band is here in force. This is Bandmaster ....

(CONDUCTOR rises.)

Say how do you do, ...

CONDUCTOR: (bowing) How -

QUEEN: That's it. I'm afraid he's very talkative too.

(HOUSE starts to dim.)

Well, they're a very nice looking lot, Oswald - Ooh, you'd better switch off, dear, the battery's running out.

1 - 1 - 18

(KING switches off torch. HOUSE out.)

QUEEN: Dear me, I do feel thirsty.

(KING nods vigorously.)

You too, dear? Well, you will talk so much. What a pity we haven't enough for a quick one in the Royal Flush - or even a slow two. (Shakes piggy bank.) No, not even as much as a sixpence. Sixpence! What a princely sum that seems. Why, I could sing a song of sixpence.

KING: And -

QUEEN: All right, we'll make it a duet. Bandmaster, can we have a duet, please - for one. (She prepares herself to sing, but the KING gets in before her.)

(MUSIC 28. "Song of Sixpence")

KING:
If I had 6d I would put it in my piggy bank;
    If I had another I would buy myself an ice;
And if I had another I would give it to a little girl,
    And she would say "Oh, thank you, sir!"
       . Now, wouldn't that be nice!
If I had 6d I would take a bus from here to there;
    If I had another I would put it in a slot;
But I haven't got a 6d and I haven't got a penny,
    And a hole in my pocket is -

QUEEN: All we've got!

KING:
If I had 6d I would go and see a Pantomime;
    If I had another I could really start to count,
'Cos if I had another and another and another,
    Then I think it would add up to a considerable amount.
If I had 6d I would only go out spending it,
    Or else I'd go and lose it and pretend it was a joke;
And that naturally leads me to the moral of this chorus -
    That we haven't got 6d, we're -

QUEEN: Just flat broke!

KING:
If I had 6d I would give it all to Charity -
    But "Charity begins at home" is my good lady's creed;
So if I had 6d I would put it in my pocket,
    And I'd feel that I was being very generous indeed.
But to say what we'd do with it is very wishful thinking,
    Or we wouldn't sing a song like this to drop you all a hint;
But the fact of the matter is, we haven't got a 6d,
    And to put the matter bluntly, we are -

QUEEN: Just plain skint!

(they exit L. with sedan. MUSIC 29. ACE puts head on L.)

ACE: Aha!

(AUDIENCE shout. He comes onstage. He has bandage round head, arm in sling and a cushion on his behind.)

Ah, how kind of you. As you see, I've repaired my head and my arm and got to the seat of the trouble elsewhere. Now I'll lie in wait for Rummy to grab the stuff for the tarts. I do hope he remembers to get some Green Shield stamps so I can nab those too. I only need ten more to get a green shield.

(Enter RUMMY D.L. with two shopping baskets containing groceries.)

Ah, here he comes. (Creeps behind L. wing.)

RUMMY: Impertinence, that's what I call it. Making me do everything on foot just because I'm a footman. Well, I've got the shopping, anyway.

ACE: (aside) Splendid. (Creeps out of hiding to behind RUMMY and raises club.)

RUMMY: Flour, jam and - oh, no butter. Blow. (Turns to go off D.L. as ACE brings club down so that he misses RUMMY and lands on his own foot.)

ACE: Yow!

RUMMY: (turning) What's that? Oh, your lordship. Did your your lordship mean to hit himself with that nasty looking object?

ACE: No! That is - yes. It's - er - a sort of endurance test to see how much pain I can stand.

RUMMY: Ah, I see your lordship failed then. (Exit RUMMY L.)

ACE: Supercilious nit! Well, I shan't fail next time. I'll nip off for a quick splint and waylay him as he comes back. (Hobbles off L.)

(MUSIC 30. PRINCE enters L. singing. He wears a costume becomingly patched with diamond - shaped patches. He carries a satchel of songs. CHORUS enter as song continues.

"Songs For Sale"

PRINCE: Songs for sale, songs for sale;
Come buy a song, I say.
Songs for sale, songs for sale;
Who'll buy a song today?

CHORUS:	What you got, what you got, what you got, what you got?
PRINCE:	A ballad.
CHORUS:	A ballad!
PRINCE:	Something ev'rybody hums To piano, bass and drums; And the lyric is a boon, Rhyming moon and June and tune.
CHORUS:	We are sure, as like as not, That you'll dispose of the whole darn lot. What you got, what you got etc?
PRINCE:	An Op'ra.
CHORUS:	An Op'ra?
PRINCE:	You sing ev'ry thing you talk To a full orchestral orch. And it doesn't matter much If you sing in double-Dutch.
CHORUS:	We are sure, etc. What you got, etc.
PRINCE:	A folk-song.
CHORUS:	A folk-song!
PRINCE:	It's accompanied by a lute And a fiddle and a flute, And it's clearly understood That the words are rather rude.
CHORUS:	We are sure, etc. What you got, etc.
PRINCE:	A romance.
CHORUS:	A romance?
PRINCE:	It's a thing a tenor sings To the sobbing of the strings Octave higher than the bass Till he's purple in the face.

1 - 1 - 21

CHORUS: We are sure, etc.
What you got, etc.

PRINCE: A pop-song.

CHORUS: A pop-song?

PRINCE: You can hear it from afar
On an amplified guitar;
And it's better for the woids
If you're born with adenoids.

CHORUS: We are sure, etc.
What you got, etc.

PRINCE: Songs for sale, songs for sale;
Come buy a song, I say.
Songs for sale, songs for sale -
Who'll buy a song today?

(Offers some of the songs from his satchel.) Now then, who'll buy a song? How about you, sir?

1st BOY CH: I haven't got my purse. (Exits with girl CH.)

PRINCE: You sir?

2nd BOY CH: I haven't got my wallet. (Exits with girl CH.)

PRINCE: And I suppose -

3rd BOY CH: (pulling out empty pockets) I'm financially embarrassed. (Exits with a girl CH.)

PRINCE: (putting music sheets away) Obviously I should have chosen a more profitable disguise. But, having been brought up as a Prince, my choice of disguises is limited - I've learnt so few useful trades. Never mind, so long as nobody knows I am really the Prince of Diamonds it will give me a chance to make up my own mind about this Princess I'm supposed to marry. If I can get into the palace, that is.

(enter PRINCESS R. in police uniform, studying a handbook)

PRINCESS: "Useful phrases. Pass along there, please". (Looking up.) Pass along there, please.(Reading.) "Now, now, no loitering". (Looking up.) Now, now no loitering.

PRINCE: I wasn't actually.

PRINCESS: Eh? Oh, I didn't mean ..... I was - er (Hastily consulting book.) "If in doubt, bend thus". (She bends her knees policemanwise, shrugs and turns to PRINCE to bend more purposefully.)

(PRINCE gives her a slight bow)

What are you bowing for?

PRINCE: I thought perhaps you were curtseying.

PRINCESS: No, I was bending thus.

PRINCE: Oh, sorry, you see, I'm so used to being curtseyed to..... Oh no, I'm not. I'm only a wandering minstrel. Er - would you like to buy a song.

PRINCESS: Not while I'm on duty. I'm a policewoman. By the way, could you tell me the time, please?

PRINCE: (laughing) Surely I should ask you that?

PRINCESS: I suppose you should, but I haven't got a watch and I'm on special security duty for the arrival of the Prince of Diamonds at noon.

PRINCE: I shouldn't worry, I think he'll be a little late. Perhaps you could help me, though. I want to get into the palace and meet the Princess.

PRINCESS: What a good idea. I mean - why?

PRINCE: Oh well .... just to see her you know and .... sell her some songs perhaps an .....

PRINCESS: And?

PRINCE: Well, I was rather keen to see whether I liked her, but I seem to have developed a sudden interest in the police.

PRINCESS: That's funny, I was very keen to meet the Prince, but I seem to have developed a sudden interest in music.

PRINCE: I wonder why?

(MUSIC 31. "Everything is Different".)

PRINCE:
All my life's gone vice versa,
May be better, may be worser.
You were really heaven-sent -
Ev'rything is different.

PRINCESS:
Please don't mind if I seem nervy,
All my world's gone topsy-turvey.
I don't know which way I went -
Ev'rything is different.

1 - 1 - 23

PRINCE: The moment that I saw you coming
I went head over heels
And now behind my ears I hear a humming
And it's strange how nice it feels.

PRINCESS: I considered me the wise 'un
Till you came on my horizon.
Now my ego's somewhat bent -

BOTH: Ev'rything is different.

Not long ago we two were strangers,
As strange as we could be.
Let's send a vote of thanks to our Arrangers
For putting us in Harmony!

There is no time like the present;
We're no longer adolescent.
You're/I'm a lady, I am/you're a gent -
So everything is different!

(They exit. MUSIC 32. ACE puts head on L.

ACE: Aha!

(AUDIENCE shout. ACE enters now with heavily bandaged foot.)

Thank you, you're very good to me. With luck this should set all right. (Looks off L.) Ah, just in time, here he comes again. (He hides behind L. wing. Enter RUMMY D.L. with 3 shopping baskets containing groceries.)

RUMMY: Whew! I'm exhausted but I have got everything.

ACE: (aside) Ah, good. (Creeps behind RUMMY raising club.)

RUMMY: The butter and the flour, jam and - oh, no salt now. Dash. (Turns to go off D.L. as ACE crashes club down onto other foot.)

ACE: Ow!

RUMMY: (turning) What's that. Ah, bad luck, your lordship. Failed your test again, eh? (He runs off D.L.)

ACE: What a martyr to me cause I am. (Hobbling L.) At least they'll match up nicely, and I'm bound to get him next time. (He hobbles off L.)

(MUSIC 33. MERLOUT rushes out of Den L. clasping hands over ears.)

1 - 1 - 24

MERLOUT: It's going to bang! I know it! It's going to go bang! (Waits crouched in C.)

MERLIN: (off L.) Boy, Boy. Where's that apprentice? Boy!

MERLOUT: Mr. Merlin!

MERLIN: (appearing in doorway with rolled up map) Ah, Merlout.

MERLOUT: Run, Mr. Merlin. It's going to go bang!

MERLIN: Listen, I've made a great discovery - what's going to go bang?

MERLOUT: The experiment.

MERLIN: Turning lead into gold number 905? What makes you think it's going to go bang?

MARLOUT: Well, the other nine hundred and four did.

MERLIN: So they did. (Peers off L.) And what's more so's this one. (Runs and joins MERLOUT, crouches beside him also clasping hands over ears. Slight pause then a pop off L. They exchange looks.)

MARLOUT: That's odd.

MERLIN: Yes, I can't think what went right. We'd better look and see.

MERLOUT: (as they move to Den.) You don't think .... ?

MERLIN: Oh no. It won't go bang now.

(EFFECT 2. Loud explosion off L., flinging them both down. Flowers in window box subside and grow again.)

MERLOUT: Mr. Merlin.

MERLIN: Yes, Merlout?

MERLOUT: It did go bang.

MERLIN: Good, good, my boy, that's what I like to see in an apprentice - accurate observation.. Well, now we know nine hundred and five different ways of turning lead into smithereens. That should be very useful to a yound lad like you. How old are you now?

MERLOUT: A hundred and four.

MERLIN: Is that all? Still, I'm only just five hundred and ten myself. Well, to work. Look what I've discovered - this old map made by my great-great-great-great-great-great-grandfather. He was the original Merlin, you know. We don't have to try to make gold, anymore. This shows us where to find some.

MERLOUT: Oh good. Where?

MERLIN: On the moon. (Unrolls map showing a large square labelled "Moon" on all four sides with a gold cross exactly in the middle.)

MARLOUT: That's a funny shaped moon.

MERLIN: Well, they hadn't invented the circle then. Wait a minute, it's upside down. (Turns it round) That's better. (Points to gold cross.) Now, that's where the gold is.

MARLOUT: But I've never seen a gold cross on the moon.

MERLIN: Neither have I, but then I've never looked for one. Let's have a look now.

(They peer up at the sky.)

That's funny. Here it is broad daylight and I can't see the moon, can you?

MERLOUT: No, somebody must have pinched it. Lock the skies! Someone's stolen the moon.

MERLIN: I know - we're not close enough. Stand on my shoulders. (They stand close to each other MERLIN cups hands in which MERLOUT puts a foot.) Right, up. Up!

MARLOUT: I can't.

MERLIN: Of course you can. Up!

MARLOUT: No, I can't.

MERLIN: Really, I don't know what you young centenarians are coming to. Surely you can get your other foot up this far?

MERLOUT: No, I can't.

MERLIN: Well, why not?

MERLOUT: 'Cos you're standing on it.

MERLIN: Oh. (Moves foot off MERLOUT'S) Now, Hup! (MERLOUT presses up and MERLIN sinks to his knees.)

MERLOUT: It's no good, your shoulders have shrunk. The funny thing is I saw the moon quite easily without standing on anything last night.

MERLIN: Ah, you've given me a valuable clue, my boy. I'll have to turn the sun out. (Takes out a magic wand) Now let me see what's the spell for that? Abraca - Abraca what's the next bit?

MERLOUT: Sesame?

MERLIN: Of course. (Waving wand.) Abraca Sesame, Hocus - er - Hocus what?

MERLOUT: I think it's something you buy a pig in.

MERLIN: That's it - Hocus sty. Right. Abraca, Sesame Hocus Sty. Switch the sun off in the sky. (Waves wand. Small flash. Wand turns into bunch of flowers.) Hm. (Hastily throws it off.) I've changed my mind. (Crossing to Den.) I've thought of a better way to take a look at the moon, through a telescope?

MERLOUT: Ah, yes. Er - what is a telescope?

MERLIN: How would I know? They haven't been invented yet.

MERLOUT: Do they go bang?

MERLIN: Certainly not.

(EFFECT 3. Pistol shots off L.)

Oh dear, is it sausages for lunch again?

(They exit L. MUSIC 34. ACE puts head on L.)

ACE: Aha!

(AUDIENCE shout. He comes onstage, now with both feet bandaged.)

I say you're getting better and better. Well, now's me last chance to get Rummy. Nothing must go wrong this time - the hospital's run out of bandage. (Looks off L.) Ah, here we go. (Hides behind L. wing.)

(Enter RUMMY D. L. with four empty shopping baskets.)

RUMMY: I shall have to take to my bed for the rest of the day after all this running around. Still, I've really got all the shopping at last.

ACE: (aside) Right then! (Creeps out behind RUMMY and raises club.)

RUMMY: But it was so heavy I asked them to deliver it. (Exits D.R.)

(ACE remains with club in air frozen in frustration for a moment then hurls club down so it lands on both feet)

ACE: Wowow! (Dances in pain from one foot to the other.)

(enter KING and QUEEN R.)

QUEEN: Ah, our Lord High Ace. Oh, I say, what kinky boots.

ACE: (stopping and bowing) Your Majesties.

QUEEN: Oh, don't stop dancing for us. Is that an easy step to learn?

ACE: (picking up his club) Very. You just drop this on your feet.

QUEEN: Really? We must try it, mustn't we, Oswald? (Takes club and drops it on KING'S feet.)

KING: Wow! (Hops from one foot to other.)

QUEEN: Ah yes. Very good, Oswald. Well, we'll have to have another go with this later. (Throws club to ACE. It lands on his feet.)

ACE: Wow! (Starts hopping.)

QUEEN: No, we must stop enjoying ourselves now, Ace, and prepare to greet the Prince of Diamonds. Dear me, the population's missing. Find them please, Oswald.

(KING opens his mouth. CHORUS run on L. and R.)

QUEEN: Well done, Oswald. Now we need Rummy to announce his Highness. Rummy!

(RUMMY looks R.)

RUMMY: You called, your Majesty?

QUEEN: Yes, Rummy.

RUMMY: (entering, revealing pyjama trousers on his legs) Well, I was half way to my bed.

QUEEN: Never mind, just announce the Prince and you can go the whole way.

RUMMY: (sighs crossing L.) I might just manage that. (Takes up stance.) His Royal Highness, the Prince of Diamonds.

(MUSIC 35. Enter BONZO L.)

BONZO: Wuff-wuff!

QUEEN: I feel there's been a slight hitch in the arrangements. Perhaps the police know where his Highness is. Penny!

PRINCESS: (off D.R.) Coming!

PENNY: (off D.L.)

(they enter and salute)

QUEEN: How odd, I seem to have got tuppence.

PRINCESS: (aside) Oh dear, I forgot Mother and Father would be here.

BOTH: I'd better slip away. (They run off.)

QUEEN: I suppose you haven't been drinking, Oswald?

(KING shakes head sorrowfully)

Then why am I seeing double? (Turning to where PENNY was.) Well now - (Is taken aback and swivels round to look where PRINCESS was.) There's not so much as a ha'penny now.

RUMMY: I can see the Prince, your Majesty. As a special favour, I'll announce him again.. His Royal Highness, the Prince of Diamonds.

(MUSIC 36. PRINCE, now attired as PRINCE, enters L. ALL bow and curtsey except KING and QUEEN.)

CHORUS: Hurray!

QUEEN: Welcome to the Land of Hearts.

PRINCE: (bowing) Your Majesties.

(PRINCESS creeps on D.R.)

PRINCESS: I must try and get a look at him.

PRINCE: (seeing PRINCESS, aside) Oh dear, my little policewoman. I don't want her to know who I am yet. (Hastily turns away.) I am delighted to meet your Majesties.

QUEEN: Delighted to see you - (Notices his averted head.) Is anything wrong, Prince?

PRINCE: No, no, just a slight crick.

QUEEN: Then we'd better come round there.

(CHORUS, KING, QUEEN, ACE and BONZO move round to PRINCE'S L.)

1 - 1 - 29

PRINCESS: (aside) Goodness, if he suffers from cricks in the neck perhaps he's very old. I'll try to peep at his face. (Tiptoes over to L.)

QUEEN: Now, your Highness, there's a banquet tonight -

PRINCE: (seeing PRINCESS) Oh dear. (Hastily turns head R.) So sorry - it's, er - cricked the other way.

(Everybody runs R.)

PRINCESS: Oh, how provoking. (Runs R.)

QUEEN: As I was -

(PRINCE jerks head L. ALL run L. except KING who stands panting and then looks curiously at PRINCESS, who averts her head. KING opens mouth.)

QUEEN: No, no, don't stand chatting, Oswald. Save your breath for running.

(KING shrugs and runs L.)

PRINCESS: I'd better go before mother recognises me. I'll just have to wait till tonight to see him. I wonder if he watches a lot of tennis? (Exit R.)

PRINCE: I think it's all right now.

QUEEN: I'm so glad.

BONZO: (nodding, panting) Wuff-wuff. (Flops heavily onto ACE'S toes.)

ACE: (hopping from foot to foot) Wow!

QUEEN: Not now, Ace. Save that for tonight. We're having a grand banquet to celebrate your betrothal to our duaghter, Prince, and everybody's invited.

CHORUS: Hurray!

(MUSIC 37. Reprise of opening Chorus)

ALL:
A banquet! A dinner! A party!
We have been invited to a do
I am going there as well as you
And when they announce us at the palace
We'll thank them hearty
A beanfeast! A nosh-up! A tuck in!
Even if the service isn't good
We'd go anywhere you like for food
A party, a party, a party!

<u>BLACKOUT</u>

Close traverse tabs

PART 1
Scene 2 - A FATEFUL MEETING.

Tabs.

(MUSIC 38. Bicycle bell heard off R. White spot up R. as FAIRY enters R. on a Fairy cycle, rather flustered. She stops R. C.)

FAIRY: Well, well, I'm glad that journey's done.
I've ridden here since rise of sun
O'er hill, o'er dale, through bush and mire
And through a very thorough briar;
A route that I were forc'd to take
'Cos somehow something's broke my brake.
I usually enjoy my ride.
I like to see the countryside
And always was a great one for
Fresh air and exercise galore,
Since I'm a fairy country-born
And easy modes of travel scorn.
Besides, a fairy in a bus
Looks ever so conspicuous.
'Course you may think that I'm astraddle
A rather insufficient saddle,
But really it's just right for me
'Cos it's a Fairy Cycle, see?

(Dismounts and parks bike on its stand.)

Well, now, my dears, I've work to do
For I am Fairy Guardian to
No less person than the Queen.
The one of Hearts, of course, I mean,
The Fairy Patience is my name;
I like to play a waiting game,
But thought I'd wait here near at hand
For I sense trouble in the land.
No harm's befell my charge as yet,
But somehow I'm prepared to bet,
Although prediction's not my forte,
That someone's up to something naughty.
And I could name the very chap -
The wicked Racing Demon Snap!

(EFFECT 4. Noise of powerful car approaching heard.)

I'm right: You hear that noise afar?
Well, that's the Racing Demon's car.
Twas surely him what broke my brake -
Well, tit for tat's a piece of cake!

(Screech of brakes off L. She waves wand, roar of car again and crash. MUSIC 39. Green spot up L. as DEMON limps on.)

DEMON:	So, you old bag, you want a fight?	
FAIRY:	Ah, Demon, always so polite. I thought I heard your car arrive. I hope you had a pleasant drive.	
DEMON:	Now, watch it, girl, don't push your luck. I'm fixing you to come unstuck. I'm up for "Demon of the Year", And I've a scheme that's really gear To put me way up in the charts - I shall ruin the Queen of Hearts!	
FAIRY:	You won't! Not while I'm on the scene. I'm Fairy Guardian to the Queen. You wicked -	
DEMON:	Oh, go stuff your face! I'm Demon Guardian to the Ace. And that's just where my scheme's so fab - It means I'll all your power grab As well as helping my own charge.	
FAIRY:	I fear your head's got overlarge. D'ye think that I'll just sit and snooze?	
DEMON:	You might as well, you're bound to lose. My magic's modern - electronic, My spell's are ulta-supersonic, My black art bas'd on nuclear fission.	
FAIRY:	Well, well, I like some competition, My magic doesn't sound so chronic, My spell's do good, just like a tonic, But as for all that fission, though, The only fission that I know Is what you get on seaside trips - The good old-fashioned fish'n chips.	
DEMON:	Don't try to bluff with all that jazz. I tell you, you're a been that has.	
FAIRY:	All right, we'll put it to the test. I'll prove old-fashion'd ways are best.	

(MUSIC 40. "SWING".)

DEMON: You gotta be with it, you gotta have hep,
You gotta be modern to keep in step.
You gotta belt it to make it ring -
Ev'rything has gotta swing.
I'm telling, you baby, that I'm way out,
And I'm the champ and no need to shout.
I'll do my ton and it's ring-a-ding -
Ev'rything has gotta swing.

FAIRY: I'm a shy retiring creature;
I don't shout until I burst;
Yet success is my strong feature -
I'm the one who gets home first.
Though our lives are slightly chequered -
Counterplots and ev'rything -
Mine is the unblemished record
You're the one who'll have to swing!

BLACKOUT

Open traverse tabs.

1 - 3 - 33

PART 1.

Scene 3 - THE ROYAL KITCHEN.

(Fullset. In front of rostrum, cloth, flats or ground row cut-out of kitchen backing. Detachable tap on it over a painted sink. Kitchen wing L, kitchen wing R, with practical door. Large stove L. C. with two frying pans on it. Table set diagonally R. C. with ping-pong ball and cotton wool balls on it.)

(RUMMY enters R. in a little apron with a feather duster, and carrying a shooting stick.)

RUMMY: Really, things have come to a pretty pass, just because her Majesty's going to bake some tarts I've been told to titivate the kitchen - me! Ah well. (Makes a few ineffectual dabs with duster.) There, that's made a thorough job of it, but it's worn me out. I'll have to take forty winks to recover. (Winking with alternate eyes.) One, two, three, four - Oh no, that's much too exhausting, I'll have a sleep instead. (Sits on shooting stick and immediately starts snoring. Snores die away).

(PRINCE, as Minstrel, creeps on L.)

PRINCE: Well, I've managed to get away and into my disguise again and to smuggle myself into the palace - now to try and get a glimpse of the Princess.

(RUMMY starts snoring again.)

What's that? The footman. I don't want to wake him (Creeps across R.)

(RUMMY'S head sinks lower and lower until it touches the feather duster and he awakes with a huge sneeze.)

RUMMY: What's this? An intruder!

PRINCE: No, it's all right, I'm just a Minstrel. I came to see if - er - if I could get a job playing at the banquet tonight and they told me to wait here.

RUMMY: They? What they?

PRINCE: Oh - just - they. The "they" who let me in.

RUMMY: Oh, them. Well, that's all right. (Closes eyes to sleep again.)

(PRINCE gives a sight of relief and is just about to move off.)

RUMMY: (suddenly reawaking) Just a minute, there aren't any "theys", except me, and I didn't let you in. I'd better get the police.

PRINCE: Oh, yes, please. I'm very fond of your police.

RUMMY: How disconcerting. I say, haven't I seen you before?

PRINCE: (averting head) Oh no.

RUMMY: Well, there's something very familiar about the back of your head. Ah, that Prince. But you can't be him. It's all this overwork, it's giving me dreams and you're a figment of my imagination. I'll have to have a proper lie down. Excuse me, figment.

(Exit - RUMMY L.)

PRINCE: That was lucky. Now to find the Princess. She's not likely to come into the kitchen. I'll see where this leads to.

(Exit through door R. Enter PRINCESS D. L. as herself.)

PRINCESS: Nobody about? Good. I hope I haven't been missed. I had to change back into my own clothes. It's a pity though, you meet much nicer people as a policewoman. I'm sure I shan't see that nice minstrel again.

(PRINCE backs on R.)

PRINCE: No, that's just the larder.

PRINCESS: My minstrel!

PRINCE: My policewoman!

PRINCESS: What are you doing here?

(They laugh.)

PRINCESS: Well, - er - I'm on special palace duty - in plain clothes, you see.

PRINCE: Very pretty plain clothes. As pretty as a Princess. But then, perhaps she isn't pretty.

PRINCESS: Well, if I am, I suppose she is.

PRINCE: You don't sound very sure. That's why I came here, I wanted to see for myself.

PRINCESS: Oh, you can't she's not here. Well, she is, but not completely.

PRINCE: Do you mean she's not all here?

PRINCESS: Yes. No! She's just not quite herself at the moment.

1 - 3 - 35

PRINCE: Dear me, she sounds a little odd.

PRINCESS: Well, you needn't worry, you're not the Prince.

PRINCE: Er - no. If I were, I'd want you for my Princess. I'm sure we could live happy ever after.

(MUSIC 41. "LOVERS")

PRINCE: Fairy tales begin with "Once upon a time"
And end "they lived happy ever after"

PRINCESS: Our tale began but a moment ago.
How it will end no one can know,

BOTH: But the tale is told with laughter.

PRINCE: Lovers - let's pretend we're lovers,
Let's pretend the rest of the world
   Has quite disappeared from view.

PRINCESS: We need not conceal it,
Hesitate to feel it,
Let us both assume
There is room there
For only us two.

PRINCE: Closer - keep on coming closer,
Let us make a pledge with our hearts,
For that is the way lover thrives.
Then if we both know
That both of us know
We will stay as lovers for the rest of our lives.

(They exit L. MUSIC 42. ACE puts head on R.)

ACE: Aha!

(AUDIENCE shout. He comes onstage.)

Ah good, you haven't forgotten. I've just popped in to steal the ingredients for those tarts. (Looks on table.) Curses! They're not here. Really, some people make villainy very difficult. How can things be stolen if they're not left lying around. Now, what am I going to do.

(Blackout. MUSIC 43. and Effect 5. roar of car approaching. Headlights flash onstage from L. Screech of brakes. Headlights out. Flash. DEMON spot on L, other lights up to half. DEMON is revealed apparently just getting out of a car and shutting door. Effect 6. door slam.)

ACE: I must be going off my nut;
I hear a car, the lights go phut,
And suddenly I see a bloke
Who evidently likes to smoke.
Who are you sir? (Crossing to L.)

DEMON: Now calm down pa.
Look out, you'll bump into my car.

ACE: What car? There isn't one to bump.
(Drum bonk as he evidently knocks into car and clasps leg in pain.)
OW. It's true. I'm going off my chump.

DEMON: Relax no mortal eyes can see
My magic racing Jag Mark Three.

ACE: It's magic, eh? How very rum.

DEMON: No, I'm your Demon Guardian, chum.

ACE: Well, I don't mean to offend at all,
But I don't want to go to a ball.

DEMON: That's fairy stuff, dead grotty, mate.
You'll find my style's more up to date.
I heard you wondering what to do,
So came to help you right on cue. (Produces phial.)
This little phial the tarts will fix -
Just pour it in the pastry mix.

ACE: Well, thank you, Demon, you're a gent,
What is it though? It looks like scent.

DEMON: Then it's the strangest one you've seen -
Atter of nitro glycerine,
Mixed with essence of T. N. T.
It's very concentrated, see,
And only heat will set it off
So when the tarts start baking - Boff!

ACE: Sir, you an evil genius are.

DEMON: Just stick by me then you'll go far.
Before I'm done, I promise, Mate,
You'll be the man they love to hate!

(BLACKOUT. Exit DEMON. Effect 7. Roar of car backing out and plunging forward and receding into distance. LIGHTS UP.)

1 - 3 - 37

ACE: What a devilish fine Demon. The only problem is how to get this into the pastry? Obviously I must lurk in wait until the pastry's made then pop it in. Where's a good lurking place? Of course, the larder. What a bit of a lurk! He-he-he! Fascinating sense of humour I have.

(He exits through door R. CHORUS march on L, carrying a large trick bag of flour, a large packet of butter, a packet of salt and jars of Plum, Strawberry, Blackcurrant, Apricot and Greengage jam and Lemon Curd and Mincemeat. Wooden spoons in jars. They process round table, placing the jars of jam etc., under the table and the other ingredients on it. CHORUS form a line L. as they sing.)

(MUSIC 44. "SALUTE THE QUEEN".)

CHORUS: Salute the Queen, the great tart maker,
Ingredients we herewith take her,
Here's salt and butter, here's jam and flour
And to read the recipe will only take her half an hour.

(RUMMY marches on L. carrying large box of "Rennies".)

RUMMY: In case her cooking's called in question
We've tablets too for indigestion.

ALL: A cookier cook there's never been
Than our culinary Queen.

(Music continues as KING carrying a large mixing bowl, JACK a large sieve, PENNY a tray with tart pans, and BONZO a jug and a large wooden spoon, march on in a line R. BONZO is out of step and trying to put it right. They are shortly followed by Queen with a large rolling pin under her arm like a swagger stick. She halts in C. beside RUMMY and OTHERS halt in a line R.)

RUMMY: The ingredients, your Majesty.

(QUEEN walks along CHORUS as if inspecting a line of soldiers.)

QUEEN: Thank you, Rummy, and they're as fine a body of ingredients as I've seen. (Eyeing RUMMY'S powdered wig.) You need a haircut, though.

RUMMY: I was referring to the groceries, your Majesty.

QUEEN: Ah yes, the groceries. A magnificent regiment. They may dismiss.

(MUSIC 45. as RUMMY and CHORUS march off L.)

QUEEN: (moving to behind table to C) Now, to work.

(They move behind table: KING and JACK to L. of her, PENNY and BONZO to R.)

1 - 3 - 38

QUEEN: Before we start, there's just one thing - does anybody know how to make pastry?

PENNY & JACK: No. (KING & BONZO shake head.)

QUEEN: Pity, Neither do I.

PENNY: Well, there's a recipe on this bag of flour.

QUEEN: Oh, good. Read it out, dear.

PENNY: "To make perfect pastry. Sift this packet of superb flour through a fine sieve into a basin then"-

QUEEN: Right, one step at a time. Have we got a basin?

KING: (nods and plonks basin on table)

QUEEN: Well done, Oswald. Anyone got a sieve?

JACK: Yes.

QUEEN: Is it a fine one?

JACK: Yes, it's a beauty.

QUEEN: (taking packet of flour from PENNY and placing it in sieve.) There we are then.

(JACK shakes packet to and fro in sieve.)

JACK: I don't think it'll go through the holes.

QUEEN: Never mind, we've tried. Just tip it in.

(JACK tips flour packet into basin.)
Carry on Penny.

PENNY: I can't. You've got the recipe on the flour.

QUEEN: So we have. (Takes packet from basin and gives it back to PENNY then looks in empty basin.) We don't seem to have got very far, do we? What happens next, Penny?

PENNY: Er "then". (Slight pause.)

QUEEN: Yes?

PENNY: "Then".

QUEEN: Then what?

PENNY: Then nothing. It stops there.

QUEEN: (takes packet) So it does.

JACK: (takes packet) Yes.

KING: (takes packet, turns it round and points to other side.)

JACK: (taking it back) Oh.

QUEEN: (taking packet) Of course.

PENNY: (taking packet) Ah.

QUEEN: Clever Oswald. Go on, Penny, after then.

PENNY: "Then see the next packet you buy of our superb flour for a further thrilling instalment".

QUEEN: Well, that's a fat lot of help.

(MERLIN runs in L.)

MERLIN: I say, I say, I say -

QUEEN: What is it Merlin? Has a funny thing happened to you on the way to the Palace?

MERLIN: No, a funny thing happened on our way to invent a telescope. We discovered an entirely new kind of flour.

QUEEN: Oh, good.

MERLIN: It's called self-raising.

(Effect 8. Loud explosion off L. MERLOUT leaps onstage from a height, bespattered with flour.)

Hm, it's even better than I thought.

MERLOUT: (showing tattered remains of bag) I'm afraid there's none left, Mr. Merlin.

MERLIN: What a pity. Shall we invent you some more?

QUEEN: No, we'll make do with what we've got. You don't happen to know how to make pastry, though?

MERLIN: Of course. I invented it years ago. Let me see, you sift a packet of flour into a basin.

(QUEEN quickly takes packet from PENNY puts it in sieve, JACK gives it one shake and tips it into basin.)

QUEEN, JACK: & PENNY: Then?

MERLIN: Then you turn the packet over.

KING: (does so)

MERLIN: And you read what it says on the other side.

QUEEN: You're a fat lot of help, too.

MERLOUT: Fat? That's right.

QUEEN: I beg your pardon?

MERLOUT: That's what comes next. I remember my mother used to invent pastry every Saturday and after she'd put in the flour she used to work in the fat.

JACK: Didn't she get a bit messy?

MERLOUT: I mean she worked that fat into the flour.

PENNY: But we havn't any fat - only butter.

QUEEN: Never mind let's work it in.

(KING opens trick bag of flour and QUEEN presses packet of butter in it.)

Right.

MERLOUT: Now, a large pinch of salt.

(QUEEN puts packet of salt in flour bag and KING closes it.)

Well, they're thoroughly worked in.

MERLOUT: Now, you stir in some water.

BONZO: (holding up jug) Wuff!

PENNY: Thanks, Bonzo. (She takes just and pours - it is empty.) You forgot to fill it.

BONZO: (looks round, sees tap U.C. and runs to point to it.)

1 - 3 - 41

PENNY: That's the ticket, but now you've forgotten the jug.

BONZO: (makes gesture of annoyance at his own stupidity, then has another brainwave and wrenches tap from wall and runs back with it)

QUEEN: Yes, well, you were on the right lines Bonzo, but how are we going to get some water?

MERLIN: Leave it to me. There's an old rain spell I used to know. Let me see. Er - (Takes out a wand and does a little dance as he incants.)

> "Abra-Hocus, mumbo-jumbo,
> By the pricking of my thumbo,
> Let the rain come back from Spain.
> And I can't remember the last line
>   except that somehow or other it ends in ain".

There. Now it'll start to rain.

(it starts to snow)

QUEEN: That's rain?

MERLIN: Hm, I'd forgotten it's an old Eskimo rain spell.

JACK: Wait a minute. I can get some water. (Starts running to and fro, jumping up and down and shouting.)

QUEEN: Goodness, what's the matter, Jack?

JACK: Nothing. I'm just getting excited.

QUEEN: Why?

JACK: Because when I get excited I - hic - hic!

(AUDIENCE shout. MUSIC 46. Glass rises. He runs and drinks keeping water in his mouth and moves up with distended cheeks. MUSIC 47. Glass descends)

PENNY: Oh, jolly good idea Jack. (She claps him on back causing him to spray water all over the QUEEN.)

QUEEN: Well, I'm wet enough now even if the pastry isn't.

(QUEEN starts to stir it with spoon)

PENNY: Can I have a go?

JACK: And me!

MERLIN: And me!

1 - 3 - 42

MERLOUT: And me!

BONZO: Wuff!

QUEEN: Scrum down!

(They gather round in a Rugby scrum from which KING emerges stirring vigorously and runs off L. with it. The scrum breaks up with suitable cries of "Where is it?" "Who's got it?" etc, KING strolls on L. having switched flour bag for a duplicate containing a pastry dough.

There, Oswald had it all the time. Is it ready, dear?

KING: (nods. Puts basin on table, undoes Flour bag and shakes out the dough onto the floor.)

QUEEN: Oh, Oswald, do be careful. You'll get the floor in a mess. (She retreives it and puts it on table.) Well, there's the pastry.

(MUSIC 48. ACE looks on R.)

ACE: Aha!

(AUDIENCE shout. ACE creeps on.)

(whispered) Thank you.

QUEEN: Oh dear, have we done something wrong?

ACE: Look up there!

(ALL look upwards.)

ACE: (aside) Now to put the explosive in (does so) so they don't "dough" what I am doing. He-he-he. I'm irrepressible today! (He creeps off R.)

PENNY: I say, I can't see anything, can you?

OTHERS: No. (They look down.)

QUEEN: Now I suppose we roll it out. (Rolls with prop roller to little effect.) That's not much good. Let's try pulling it.

(JACK takes one end of dough, QUEEN the other. PENNY clasps her round waist and BONZO PENNY'S waist. KING claps JACK'S waist, MERLIN JACK'S AND MERLOUT MERLIN'S.

ALL: Heave! Heave! Heave! (They pull it as far as possible.)

QUEEN: Obviously this isn't short pastry. Let's try pulling little bits off.

(they take it back to table and succeed in pulling off some small pieces which they start throwing at each other)

QUEEN: Now, now no larking - Oh I don't know it looks rather fun. (Takes frying pans from stove and hands one to KING) Serve, Oswald!

(KING serves ping-pong ball. They play a few strokes, then he serves a cotton wool ball, which QUEEN knocks into Auditorium and continues doing so as fast as he serves them, ending by picking up a handful and throwing them at AUDIENCE)

Right, back to work. Put the pastry in the pans. (They do so.)
Now for the jam. What kind do you think, Oswald?

(KING brings up and plonks on the table the Blackcurrant jam pot.)

Blackcurrant - hm.

BONZO: (brings up and plonks on table apricot)

QUEEN: Apricot, eh?

JACK: (bringing up jar) No, Strawberry.

PENNY: (bringing up jar) Greengage.

MERLIN: (bringing up jar) Lemon curd.

MERLOUT: (bringing up jar) Mincemeat.

QUEEN: Oh no, it must be jam. (Bringing up jar) I plump for plum.

(argumentative advocacy from others)

QUEEN: All right, we'll each make some of our own.

(they start to spoon out of their jams. JACK and PENNY are a little slow so KING and BONZO fill two tarts each)

JACK: Hey, that was one of mine.

PENNY: And that was one of mine, Bonzo.

JACK: Well, I shall put that on yours.

PENNY: And I'll put that on yours.

(a fight developes involving them all flicking jams at each other with spoons, using the tarts like custard pies, etc. This can be built up and made as "mucky" as desired.)

1 - 3 - 44

QUEEN: Stop! Do let's get them in the oven - what there is of them.

(they put the remains in the oven)

Well, I can think of a lot of other things I'd rather make than tarts in future.

OTHERS: So can we.

(MUSIC 49. "Something Stirred")

ALL: Down in the kitchen something stirred,
We'll tell you exactly what occurred.

KING: A goulash is the dish for me,
If you are very Hungary.

OTHERS: Ooh!

(QUEEN opens her mouth to sing)

ALL: Down in the kitchen something stirred
And her Majesty didn't say a word.

Down in the kitchen something stirred,
We'll tell you exactly what occurred.

KING: A goulash, etc.

MERLIN: I used some sawdust to make a pudden
But to eat it people simply wooden.

OTHERS: Ooh!

(QUEEN opens her mouth to sing)

ALL: Down in the kitchen something stirred
And her Majesty didn't say a word.

Down in the kitchen something stirred,
We'll tell you exactly what occurred.

KING: A goulash, etc.

MERLIN: I used some, etc.

MERLOUT: I bashed a steak with a great big mallet,
Which I eat with a salad dressed by a valet.

(QUEEN opens her mouth to sing)

1 - 3 - 45

ALL: Down in the kitchen something stirred
And her Majesty didn't say a word.
Down in the kitchen something stirred
We'll tell you exactly what occurred.

KING: A goulash, etc.

MERLIN: I used some, etc.

MERLOUT: I bashed, etc.

PENNY: To make a swiss roll is a thrill,
You start him from the top of a hill.

OTHERS: Ooh!

(QUEEN opens mouth to sing)

ALL: Down in the kitchen something stirred
And her Majesty didn't say a word.
Down in the kitchen something stirred,
We'll tell you exactly what occurred.

KING: A goulash, etc.

MERLIN: I used some, etc.

MERLOUT: I bashed, etc.

PENNY: To make a, etc.

JACK: To get some Cerebos and Exide free
I committed assault and battery.

OTHERS: Ooh!

(QUEEN opens her mouth to sing)

ALL: Down in the kitchen something stirred
And her Majesty didn't say a word.

(stove has started to glow red and gets brighter and brighter)

QUEEN: Beasts! (Leans on stove.) Aah! I didn't know this was a red stove.

JACK: It wasn't.

MERLIN: It's getting redder!

MERLOUT: And redder!

PENNY: Do you think it's all right?

QUEEN: It must be, I only set it at number seven. I mean, what could possibly go wrong with it?

(EFFECT 9. Loud explosion. Lights flicker. Stove flies in pieces. ALL run off R, except QUEEN.)

My tarts, my tarts! Where are my tarts? (A number of charred tarts land at her feet. She kneels.) Oh, they're ruined! And so am I. So's the whole country! The betrothal can't take place and we're ruined!

(MUSIC 50. BONZO enters R. with a bone in his mouth, which he offers her. her.)

Oh, Bonzo. That's very sweet of you, but we can't very well seal a royal betrothal with a dog bone.

BONZO: (rubs head against her comfortingly)

QUEEN: Thank you for trying to help, though, Bonzo.

(He pads softly off U.R. Tabs close slowly behind QUEEN and lights dim. Fly in Scene 4 frontcloth)

But I'm afraid nobody can help. I'm just a silly bungling old chatterbox and I've ruined everything.

(WHITE FLASH R. Fairy's spot up R. MUSIC 51. Enter Fairy R.)

FAIRY: Now, now, my dear, don't take on so;
Things aren't as bad as that, you know.

QUEEN: Good gracious! How did you appear?

FAIRY: Well, I'm your Fairy Guardian, dear.

QUEEN: A fairy? Do I sleep or wake?

FAIRY: I'll help, my dear, your tarts to bake.
Just come with me and hand in hand
We'll whisk away to Fairyland.
You'll find that I don't speak at random,
For I have brought a Fairy tandem!

(MUSIC 52. As they exit R.)

BLACKOUT.

Open traverse tabs.

1 - 4 - 47

PART 1

SCENE 4 - THE PALACE PORTRAIT GALLERY

(Frontcloth of Gallery of portraits of former Kings and Queens of Hearts. Space between pictures L.C. with notice - "WATCH THIS SPACE".)

(MUSIC 53. ACE puts head on L.)

ACE: Aha!

(AUDIENCE shout. He enters with a large picture frame.)

Ah, music to my ears. I feel I'm really beginning to deserve your kind support, too. My dastardly scheme is coming along very nicely. I've already bought a frame for Jack's portrait to go up there. (Points to space.) I should like to see him hung. Now I've ruined the tarts they'll have to call off the Princess's betrothal to the Prince of Diamonds, so she might as well marry Jack at once. I hope he doesn't raise any objections about not being in love or any unimportant details like that.

(Enter JACK R.)

JACK: Father, Father, Father, I'm in love.

ACE: Really? How convenient.

JACK: I'm in love with the prettiest -

ACE: Yes, she is quite pretty.

JACK: The dearest.

ACE: Ah, expensive taste, eh? Well, never mind.

JACK: And the best girl in all the world. She may be poor -

ACE: Well, I've seen to that. Unfortunately, she's also honest, but I daresay we can change that.

JACK: She may even be humble.

ACE: Oh, come, come, she _is_ the Princess of Hearts.

JACK: Yes, she _is_ the - no she isn't. I'm not in love with the Princess. I'm in love with the Police.

ACE: What?

JACK: I'm in love with Penny.

ACE: A member of our family in love with the police! How dare you? How dare you not blot the family escutcheon? And we've got a lovely escutcheon - a two-faced double-cross on a bar sinister. Why do you think I've spent so much time ruining the King and Queen?

JACK: I don't know. Why have you spent so much time ruining - ?

ACE: (looking off L.) Soft!

JACK: I'm not soft.

ACE: I mean we are not alone.

JACK: Why, who else has been trying to ruin -

ACE: Belt up! Here come the Sorcerers. I want to hear what they're up to. Stand aside, boy.

(JACK moves R.)

Further aside.

(JACK moves R. further)

Further aside still

(JACK exits R.)

That's it.

JACK: (putting on head) Well, I'm offside here.

ACE: That's where I want you. Now, where can I hide? Ah, I have it. (To AUDIENCE.) Don't let on! (He holds up frame and stands in front of space L.C.)

(MUSIC 54. MERLIN enters L. closely followed by MERLOUT.)

MERLIN: Merlout! Merlout! Where are you, boy?

MERLOUT: Here, Mr. Merlin.

(They stop in front of ACE)

MERLIN: Oh, well no wonder I couldn't see you. A most extraordinary thing has happened, Merlout. That telescope we invented - it's worked! I saw the moon quite clearly and there is gold there.

ACE: Gold!

MERLIN: Yes, gold. On the moon.

ACE: On the moon!

1 - 4 - 49

MERLIN: On the Moon. And I've run up a little invention to get us there. I've called it a space ship.

ACE: A space ship!

MERLIN: A space - don't keep repeating everything I say. It should be finished tonight. We'll nip to the moon and get the gold by tomorrow. Won't their Majesties be pleased?

ACE: Not if I can help it.

MERLIN: You're acting in a very strange way, Merlout. Perhaps it's time you had a little break. I'll invent tea.

(They start to move off L.)

No, I've had a better idea. I'll invent opening time.

MERLOUT: Oh, yes. (Moving to catwalk.) I've invented something too.

MERLIN: What's that?

MERLOUT: (going into Auditorium) A quick way to get there.

(MERLIN follows him and they exit to Bar. ACE lowers frame and puts it off L.)

ACE: Jack!

(JACK enters R.)

Did you hear that?

JACK: Yes.

ACE: If they get gold from the moon it will ruin everything. We must put a stop to it. But how?

(BLACKOUT. MUSIC 55. EFFECT 10. Roar of DEMON'S car approaching, screech of brakes, door slam. DEMON'S spot up L. and lights to low. DEMON enters L. JACK is wrapped round R. pros arch clinging to it in terror)

ACE: The very bloke!

JACK: Aah, help, old Nick!

DEMON: What's wrong with him, then?

JACK: I - hic - hic!

(AUDIENCE shout. MUSIC 56. Glass rises. He drinks. MUSIC 57. Glass descends)

1 - 4 - 50

JACK: Thanks. That gave me a nasty scare.

ACE: Don't fuss. I'm sure my good friend there comes but to help us.

DEMON: That's right, Pop.
This moon jaunt you can eas'ly stop -
Just go and grab the gold yourself.

ACE: Well, I'm all for some extra pelf,
But at the risk of sounding trite,
Just how and when?

DEMON: Simple - tonight -
Go to the banquet, see, and then
Both slope off to the Sorc'rers's Den -
Hijack the space ship - off you go.

ACE: Hi what did you say?

DEMON: Hijack.

JACK: Hullo.

ACE: You mean we pinch it?

DEMON: That's my boy.

JACK: It sounds to me a naughty plot.

ACE: Dear me, it's really very sad,
My son just simply won't be bad.
Could you not help this lack to cure?
and teach him villainy?

DEMON: Why, sure.
The modern way of learning it
Is with an instant villain's kit.

(Claps hands. Whizz whistle. Large box, labelled "INSTANT VILLAIN'S KIT" slides on L. DEMON opens it. He and ACE take out some of the things mentioned)

DEMON: There's a handy cosh for a wages snatch.

ACE: And a brick. For a smash and grab raid?

DEMON: Natch. Assorted jemmies for cracking cribs -

ACE: Moustaches for twirling -

DEMON: Foolproof fibs, Deceptive disguises -

1 - 4 - 51

ACE: Dastardly schemes,
And curses arrang'd in voluble streams -

DEMON: Forgery nibs -

ACE: And a special boon,
For wicked thoughts, a huge balloon.
Well, with this he'll learn in a trice
To tread the righteous paths of vice.

(MUSIC 58. "What's Evil". Close traverse tabs slowly during number and fly out front cloth)

ACE: Here's lesson number one
On being evil, my son.

DEMON: What's fraud? (JACK shrugs.)

If you sell a dozen eggs to somebody,
And you say they're the finest to be had,
Yet a couple smell most atrociously -
What would that be?

JACK: (thinks) Too bad.

ACE: What's arson? (JACK shrugs.)

If on purpose you should set a house on fire,
While you're taking shelter from a storm,
And it burns and burns and burns and burns and burns -
What would that be?

JACK: (thinks) Nice and warm.

DEMON: If you went into a den of vice,
And you kiss'd a girl not once but twice -
What would that be?

JACK: Ever so nice.

ACE AND DEMON: Don't be such a thick-head,
That's not being wicked!

DEMON: What's theft? (JACK shrugs.)

If you take a shilling from a little boy,
Then you take another just for kicks,
Then you take a sixpence from your Auntie Lil -
What would that be?

JACK: (thinks) Two and six.

(DANCE)

ACE: What's murder ? (JACK shrugs.)
Farmer Brown's bull is worth about a thousand pounds,
And you know it's value to the full,
Then you put a bomb in its feeding box -
What would that be?

JACK: (thinks) A-bomb-in-abull!

BLACKOUT

Open traverse tabs

PART 1

SCENE 5 - A CROWDED CORNER OF FAIRYLAND

(Full set. Groundrow cut-out of a stylised country landscape at back. Hillock U. C. in which is an opening for salt mine. U. L. wing to which is attached water mill piece to appear later. This can either be hinged to swing on, or it can be a separate piece slid on behind the wing. The mill wheel can be made to turn by fixing it to an axle with a handle which is worked from behind. Wooden bucket by wing. Below this low cut-out to conceal trick plum tree, on nylon line so that it can be pulled up from offstage. Detachable plums on tree. U. R. a doll's house sort of exterior on small truck to swing round to reveal kitchen interior later, with stove and small table with pastry making utensils set on it. Below this low cut-out to conceal trick wheat. This should be a number of canes fitted into a batten. To begin they are bent over to lie on the ground compressing a spring attached to the batten and are held down by a line across them so that when this is released they will spring up. The tops of the canes have detachable wheat ears. A traverse line about half-way back to work cut-out cow. This is suspended by nylon lines attached to runners and the runners are pulled on, line a curtain, by a line operated offstage)

(MUSIC 59. Ballet. PATIENCE enters summoning CHORUS as Fairies. Short dance with them, then she dismisses them and brings on QUEEN OF HEARTS in a balletic version of her costume. Pas de deux for FAIRY and QUEEN. After this PATIENCE summons 1st FAIRY who enters wearing something suggestive of a farmer. She plants wheat seed D. L. waves her hands spell like over it and trick wheat springs up. While she is harvesting wheat ears, PATIENCE calls forth 2nd FAIRY who enters in something suggestive of a Miller. She conjures up a water mill U. L. 1st FAIRY brings her wheat to put into mill. Mill wheel turns and packet marked "FLOUR" comes out. As wheel turns 1st FAIRY "fills" wooden bucket with "water". PATIENCE summons 3rd FAIRY who plants a plum stone D. L. and conjures up trick plum tree with detachable plums. As she gathers plums PATIENCE summons 4th FAIRY who wears something suggestive of a dairy maid and who carries a wooden bucket and a milking stool and leading a cut-out cow from R. She milks cow and exits L. with it leaving bucket onstage for 5th FAIRY who enters also as a dairy maid, with a churn into which she pours milk and "churns" it into a ready wrapped packet marked "BUTTER". FAIRIES now offer the water, flour, butter and plums to PATIENCE, who, as an afterthought, hastily summons 6th FAIRY who enters with a little pick and goes into salt mine U. C. and hews out a packet of "CEREBOS". PATIENCE moves with QUEEN to house and waves wand. Truck swings round to reveal kitchen interior. Under guidance of PATIENCE, who dons a cook's hat, the QUEEN swiftly mimes making some jam from plums then making pastry and baking tarts)

(All the previous action can have been interrupted from time to time, if desired, by the DEMON, possibly with attendant IMP or IMPS; though naturally, all his efforts such as putting a blight on the wheat and the plum tree, stopping the water mill, turning the milk sour would be thwarted by the FAIRIES)

(The tarts are taken from oven. PATIENCE and QUEEN lead them in triumph to C. FAIRIES flank themselves around them)

QUEEN: At my call the ballet dances,
Terpsichore has been my aid.
Despite some contrary circumstances,
I declare these tarts well and truly made.

CURTAIN

(Curtain up. Tableau with the tarts held victoriously aloft. DEMON and IMPS, if any, in a chagrinned fist-shaking group L.)

CURTAIN

(MUSIC 60. Entr'acte.)

2 - 6 - 55

PART 11

SCENE 6 - THE ROYAL BANQUET

(Full set. Palace decor. Cut-out ground row of pillars and arches along back of rostram. Seat in C, possibly round base of a pillar)

(CHORUS, all as girls in ball dresses, discovered)

(MUSIC 61. "Girls")

CHORUS: We are shy retiring young ladies,
Gay and debonair,
You think that nothing much happens
Underneath our hair.
But because we're feminine creatures
Looking far from strong,
If you're thinking of taking advantages -

(PENNY enters)

PENNY: Boy, you're wrong!

(CHORUS take out policewomen's caps from their reticules and put them on)

ALL: 'Cos we're the pride of the force of women P.C.'s.
We are on a job today.
We're armed to the teeth with a thousand

(CHORUS take truncheons from their garters)

Of getting our own way.

PENNY: We are prepared for anything you do,
Are you all set for a session of Judo?

ALL: From the Women P.C.'s Corps.

CHORUS: We're a group of simpering ninnies,
Not much use at all,
We appear for just decoration
At the Royal Ball,
But appearances are deceptive,
Looks can sometimes lie.
If you're thinking of trying a something
Boy, just try!

'Cos we're the pride of the Force of Women P.C.'s
And we've got a job to do.
So if there's a man to be put in his place
It might easily be you.

2 - 6 - 56

PENNY: So if you are thinking of wrecking the party
You might walk into a spot of Karate!

ALL: From the women's P.C. Corps.

(PENNY exits R. RUMMY enters U.L. carrying a staff in his R. hand. He stops L.C. facing front with his R. foot forward.)

RUMMY: (bangs staff twice near his R. foot and is about to bang a third time) Ah, you thought I was going to bang it on that foot, didn't you? (Transfers staff to his L. hand and swivels so that he brings his L. foot forward.) Not likely. (Brings staff down on L. foot.) Ow! I don't know why I keep using this thing. I make the same mistake every time. Still, it's an occupational hazard, I suppose. (Clears throat.) Ladies and - how very odd, we usually have an assortment. Oh well, ladies and ladies, His Excellency the -

(MUSIC 62. ACE puts head on D.L.)

ACE: Aha! (AUDIENCE shout) Ah, in splendid form after your rest, I see. I thought we'd just get that over before I make a more formal appearance. Back in a moment. (Disappears.)

RUMMY: What a noisy lot of guests. Where had I got to? Oh, yes. His Excellency the Lord High Ace of Hearts.

(CHORUS curtsey as ACE enters U.L. He bows)

ACE: Ladies and - well, what a pleasant surprise. Er - hm. I have a grave announcement to make. Her Majesty, the Queen, regrets that she has been unable to make any tarts.

RUMMY: (as he enters) Make way for the Royal Tarts!

ACE: What!

(MUSIC 63. Enter PENNY, holding out truncheon and BONZO bearing plate of tarts. CHORUS fall in on either side of him holding truncheons at the ready)

Curses! My plots gone to pot' (Aside to AUDIENCE.) I'll go and have a quick brood and hatch another one. Never fear, I'll dispose of those tarts somehow before the betrothal takes place. (He exits D.L. RUMMY bangs three times with staff in L. hand, watching very carefully for 3rd bang, expels breath with satisfaction and transfers staff to R. hand and inadvertently bangs it on R. toe.)

RUMMY: Ow! (Sighs.) It's just not my day. Ladies, and - (Takes a quick look to see that there are still only ladies.) Ladies.

BONZO: Wuff!

RUMMY: And dog. Prepare to receive their Majesties, the King and Queen of Hearts.

(MUSIC 64. BONZO and RUMMY bow and PENNY and CHORUS curtsey to R. Pause. RUMMY looks up and peers off R. KING trots on L. touches RUMMY on shoulder and points L. to indicate that he and QUEEN are on L. side, then trots off L. RUMMY sighs and ALL shuffle round in their bent and curtsied positions. MUSIC 65. KING and QUEEN enter U. L. and come C. being very gracious. KING wears a high pointed crown)

QUEEN: Ladies and -

(KING trips and rams QUEEN in rear with crown)

Oswald! (Rubbing behind.) Do be careful of my Royal dignity. Now where was I?

KING: (indicates point of crown)

QUEEN: Yes, but before that. Ah, I was making your speech. Yes, ladies and - (Looks round.)

(KING eyes CHORUS, rubbing hands gleefully)

QUEEN: Oswald! Did you make out the invitation list, by any chance?

PENNY: Special security guard, your Majesty.

QUEEN: Oh no, Oswald's not that bad. Oh, I see. You mean they are for the tarts. How splendid, and with Bonzo to help I'm sure the tarts are in safe - er - paws.

BONZO: (very bucked, bows and nearly upsets them all off the plate)

PENNY: (just managed to save them) Bonzo! (She takes plate from him.)

QUEEN: Thank goodness for that. I couldn't have done all that ballet dancing again. You'd better keep them somewhere safe until we're ready for them, Penny.

PENNY: Yes, your Majesty. (She exits D.R. BONZO follows.)

QUEEN: Well, ladies, my husband and I are delighted to welcome you to our banquet to celebrate the betrothal of our dear daughter to the Prince of Diamonds - that is if he turns up. We haven't seen him since he arrived yesterday. Any sign of him, Rummy?

RUMMY: No, your Majesty. (On shaking head he glances off R.) Yes, your Majesty. (He taps heavily twice EVERYONE turns expecting the third and he then gives a light little tap.) His Royal Highness the Prince of Diamonds.

2 - 6 - 58

(MUSIC 66. Enter PRINCE U.R. CHORUS curtsey. RUMMY bows)

PRINCE: (bowing) Your Majesties. (He is rather glum.)

QUEEN: Ah, Prince. We were getting a bit worried about you. You look a bit worried yourself. Is your neck troubling you again?

PRINCE: No, your Majesty.

QUEEN: Well, we'll introduce you to your future bride. That'll cheer you up.

PRINCE: (glummer that ever) Yes, your Majesty.

QUEEN: Ah, you're just like Oswald when we first met. Isn't he, Oswald.

KING: (nods gloomily)

QUEEN: Dear Oswald, he hasn't changed a bit. Rummy, summon the Princess, please.

RUMMY: Very well, your Majesty. But it is two flights up. It's very tiring shouting all that way. (Turns putting hand up to mouth.)

QUEEN: Oh no, Rummy, do save your voice.

RUMMY: (turning back) Thank you, your Majesty.

QUEEN: Not at all. Use your legs instead.

RUMMY: I was afraid your Majesty would say that. (Exit R.)

QUEEN: Rummy's always so obliging. Don't worry Prince, the Princess will be here in a jiffy.

PRINCE: Oh dear, will she? Perhaps, I could meet a policewoman first? I mean - some of the other guests. (Backing to R.) Yes, I'm sure I should. Don't worry. See you - may be, I mean - soon. But - Well, don't hold anything up for me, will you? (Exit R.)

QUEEN: How very odd. Still, if he wants to see a policewoman you girls had better go with him.

CHORUS: Yes, your Majesty. (They exit R.)

QUEEN: Don't be too eager, though. He's spoken for, you know, Oswald, you keep an eye on them.

KING: (nods eagerly and rushes off R.)

QUEEN: (looks round) Now, there's nobody left to keep an eye on him. (Sits on R. of circular seat.) Never mind. Oswald prefers a mature woman like myself. Not that I'm all that mature. In fact, I'm only thirty-five. Well - would you settle for thirty-five and a half? Now, where's that child got to, Rummy's a long time fetching her.

(PRINCESS creeps on U. L.)

PRINCESS: Nobody about? Good. Then perhaps I could run away. But where to? My lovely Minstrel's disappeared now. Oh, what am I to do?

QUEEN: Well, try having a little chat with me, dear.

PRINCESS: Mother!

(QUEEN pats seat beside her)

(moving up to sit by QUEEN) But I don't think you'd understand. You see I'm in love. I fell in love at first sight.

QUEEN: Oh, that's very dangerous. Although I must admit it was just like a fairy story when your father and I first met.

PRINCESS: Was it, Mother? Oh, do tell me.

QUEEN: I was going to dear, don't worry. Once upon a time there was a beautiful young Princess - well, quite a nice-looking young princess - all right, a <u>young</u> princess who met a hands- a <u>young</u> Prince and they fell in love at first sight.

PRINCESS: Really?

QUEEN: Yes. The Prince fell in love with her younger sister and she fell in love with his older brother. But the younger sister and brother were already betrothed to each other which meant that the young Prince and Princess were stuck with each other. And so you see we lived happily ever after.

PRINCESS: But how could you?

QUEEN: Well, we were the younger sister and elder brother.

PRINCESS: What about the other two?

QUEEN: Oh, they had a terrible time, they just <u>lived</u> ever afterwards. But it shows how dangerous love at first sight can be. And when it comes marriage well - what do you expect from marriage?

(MUSIC 67. "Love Story")

PRINCESS: There's just one man that I want in my lifetime.
One who is proud and strong
Someone who'll make the walls
The house where I belong.
Then will I fill it with laughter of children
Then will the air be wine.
Then will we own the whole of the world,
Me and this man of mine.

(The all move U. L. KING and PRINCE enter R.)

KING: When a woman comes into your life
You must make no attempt to evade her.
She is seeking fulfilment of dreams
For that is the way God made her.
But don't think she is selfish in this
That you'll end up by being possessed
You'll receive all the treasurers most dear to your heart
And you are the one who is blessed.

(KING and QUEEN draw the unwilling couple together. MUSIC continues under dialogue)

BOTH: (turning in) - YOU! (They move to each other.) But - I thought - you - (They laugh.)

PRINCE: Never mind - you are my Princess after all.

PRINCESS: And you're my Prince.

PRINCE AND PRINCESS: Lovers - now we know we're lovers,
Let us make a pledge with our hearts
For that is the way love thrives.

PRINCE, PRINCESS, KING AND QUEEN: Now that we/you both know that both of us/you know
We/you will stay as lovers for the rest of our/your lives.

QUEEN: You see, Oswald, it was love at first sight.

KING: (nods happily)

QUEEN: Now all we've got to do is have the official betrothal ceremony then we'll get the handsome gift, we'll be able to repay the Ace - and all our troubles will be over. What more could we want?

KING: (indicates that he would like a drink)

QUEEN: Oswald, you have a one track mind. And a very good track it is, too.

(KING and QUEEN hasten off R.)

(Enter RUMMY U. L.)

RUMMY: Well, really, I tire myself out going up two flights of stairs to look for her Highness and she's down here all the time. Never mind, I'll treat myself to a little zizz. (He sits on R. side of seat almost out of view, starts snoring immediately and is then silent. ACE puts head on D. L.)

ACE: Aha!

(MUSIC 68. AUDIENCE shout. He enters hands behind back)

Thank you - you do wonders for my confidence. Well, master of resource that I am, I've come up with a new plan - Jack shall steal the tarts.

(Enter JACK R.)

Ah, Jack, how fortunate. I want you to do something for me.

JACK: Yes, of course, father, what is it?

ACE: Steal the tarts.

JACK: But I don't like tarts.

ACE: Neither do I but they stand between me and a kingdom. I shall be at the Sorcerers's Den as we originally planned for our trip to the moon. Steal the tarts and bring them to me there.

JACK: But Penny's looking after the tarts. She'll recognise me.

ACE: Not in this long black cloak, black hat and black mask I happen to have behind my back. (Produces them and a water pistol.) Also this.

JACK: Oh no - I might kill her.

ACE: You'll have to drown her then. It's a water pistol. It's just to threaten with.

JACK: (taking it) Oh. How does it work? (Squuzes it into ACE'S face)

ACE: (resignedly) Like that.

(RUMMY awakes with a snort)

(sotto voice) What's that? Is there somebody there? (He and JACK move up round L. side of pillar.)

RUMMY: I thought I heard voices.

(RUMMY comes below pillar to L. side as they get to R. side)

RUMMY: Nobody there.

ACE: Nobody there.

(ACE and JACK and RUMMY back towards each other below pillar and almost collide, but RUMMY moves forward and comes to R. side again as ACE and JACK turn and go forward to L. side)

It's all right. Now don't forget steal the tarts -

RUMMY: (aside) There is somebody!

ACE: And bring them to me in the Sorcerers's Den. (They move L.)

RUMMY: (aside) Thieves! Dare I look? No, they might see me.

ACE: And remember what I told you disguise yourself as to get to the Den.

(They exit L.)

RUMMY: Goodness, they were planning to steal the tarts! I'd inform the police at once, if only it didn't mean a long walk.

(Enter PENNY R. with tarts and BONZO U.S. of her)

Ah, I shan't have to bother.

PENNY: Keep an eye out all round, Bonzo.

BONZO: Wuff! (Nods.)

(Just as PENNY draws level with RUMMY BONZO rushes across in front of her looking all round. This causes her to pull up sharply nearly precipitating tarts from plate)

PENNY: Oh, Bonzo! I'm afraid he's rather over enthusiastic.

RUMMY: And well he may be, miss. I've just overheard someone plotting a plot to steal those tarts.

PENNY: No!

RUMMY: Yes "Steal them and bring them to me at the Sorcerers's Den" I heard one say to the other.

PENNY: Two of them, eh? Do you know who they were, Rummy?

RUMMY: No, I purposely kept myself hidden to discover as much as possible. "Ah, little do they know," I thought, "that their wicked scheme is already doomed. For even littler do they know that listening to their every word is me, Rummy who is really the deadly efficient secret agent, brother of James Bond - Basildon Bond!

PENNY: Gosh, are you, Rummy?

RUMMY: No, not really. But we all have our dreams, don't we? Excuse me, I think I'll have a lie down after all the excitement. (Exit L.)

PENNY: Golly, how super! A real crime at last. I'll summon the Security Guard. (Puts tarts on seat. Blows whistle, it is silent.) Oh blast, I can't blast. I must remember to put the pea back. Well, we'll tackle it alone, eh, old fellow? You remember how I taught you to capture a man, Bonzo?

BONZO: (shakes head)

PENNY: You must do, Bonzo. You jumped up, grabbed my arm and pinioned me to the ground, remember?

BONZO: (nods, remembering)

(JACK enters in cloak, hat and mask, holding out pistol)

JACK: Hands up, your money or your tarts!

PENNY: (growls menacingly, leaps, grabs her arm and pinions her to the ground)

PENNY: Bonzo, we're not training now. Get him, not me.

JACK: No, don't make a move or I fire - like this. (He is holding it the wrong way round and squeezes it in own face.) Ugh! I knew I'd make a muck of it. I - hic! hic!

(AUDIENCE shout. MUSIC 69. Glass rises, he runs and drinks. BONZO releases PENNY and she sits up. MUSIC 70. Glass subsides)

Ta.

PENNY: Hic? Then it must be - Ooer. (She faints into BONZO'S arms.)

JACK: Oh dear, she's fainted!

BONZO: (fans her with paws)

JACK: Well, at least it's given me a chance to steal the tarts. (Takes them from seat.) But what can I do about -

(Voices are heard approaching off R.)

JACK: Ooh, nothing, I must get away at once! (Runs off L.)

BONZO: (drops PENNY and runs barking after JACK. Realises he has dropped PENNY and runs back to her then runs R. barking for help to L.)

(Enter KING and QUEEN with PRINCE and PRINCESS from R. and CHORUS L. and R. RUMMY enters L.)

QUEEN: Ah, Bonzo's getting all excited about the betrothal. Rummy make sure everyone's here so we can start. Really, what an inconvenient place for Penny to go to sleep.

BONZO: (shakes head frienziedly and gives a rather over-dramatic impression of someone fainting)

PRINCESS: I think he means she's fainted, Mother.

QUEEN: What? We must bring her round. (She and PRINCE help PENNY up.) What's the matter, dear.

PENNY: The tarts - the tarts.

QUEEN: It's all right dear, Oswald's just going to call for them.

KING: (opens mouth)

QUEEN: You see, he is calling for them.

PENNY: But it's no good.

QUEEN: No, I know it isn't really. But we get the idea.

PENNY: You don't understand. The tarts have gone.

QUEEN, PRINCE and PRINCESS: Gone?

PENNY: Yes, they've been stolen clean away!

(General reaction)

QUEEN: Then they must be found and his Majesty will give the culprit a thorough beating with his own fair hand, won't you Oswald? But whatever happens - the tarts must be found!

(MUSIC 71)

QUEEN:	(spoken under music)	
	I'm Queen of Hearts and I'm a cook,	
	I made some tarts and they've been took -	
	To make some pastry was my goal,	
	I made some tarts and they've been stole.	
	Find them!	
CHORUS:	Yes, your Majesty.	
QUEEN:	Find them!	
CHORUS:	Yes, your Majesty.	
QUEEN:	Find them!	
CHORUS:	Yes, your Majesty.	
QUEEN:	Find them!	
CHORUS:	Yes, your Majesty.	

BLACKOUT

(Close traverse tabs and drop in Scene 7 frontcloth, if used)

2 - 7 - 66

PART 11
SCENE 7 - ON THE WAY TO THE DEN

(Tabs or Street Scene frontcloth. If cloth is used open traverse tabs as soon as convenient during scene.)

(MUSIC 72. ACE puts head on R.)

ACE: Aha!

(AUDIENCE shout)

Thanks, fans. (He enters putting a tall hat like MERLIN'S and wearing a similar costume.) Surprise, surprise! I bet you thought I was Merlin. a brilliant notion, eh? Now nobody will realise it is really me hurrying to the Sorcerer's Den. What a clever chap I am - in fact, I'm a constant Sorcerer of delight to myself. He-he-he! I'm sorry, I can't help being so funny. I kill myself. (Walks into pros. arch L. I practically did. (Exit L. Slight pause enter KNAVE R. in a costume similar to MERLOUT'S but the hat is too large and keeps slipping over his eyes. He is rather breathless and carries the plate of tarts)

JACK: I've got away but I'm sure they'll catch me. (Hat slips over eyes.) They have. They've thrown a sack over me. (Pushes hat back.) Oh no, it's this. It gets me so flustered and - hic - hic - hic!

(AUDIENCE shout. MUSIC 73. Glass rises, he runs and drinks. MUSIC 74. Glass descends)

Thanks. I'm supposed to be disguised as Merlout, but I'm not cut out for this sort of thing, you know. (Flaps an overlong sleeve.) I don't think this was cut out for me, either. (Hat slips, pushes it back.) This hat's downright dangerous - I could kill myself in an outfit like this. (Hat slips Crashes into pros. arch L.) You see, I nearly did.

QUEEN: (off R.) Oswald! Searchers! Follow me!

JACK: Ooh, here they come! (Runs off L. CHORUS run on R. giggling, closely followed enthusiastically by KING. A little gap then QUEEN enters.)

QUEEN: Oswald! I said follow me. (Moves to R. of KING. They should be flanked by 2 CHORUS girls on either side and 2 behind them.) We'll never find the tarts if we don't organise ourselves. Now, what were you thinking of doing, Oswald?

(KING looks at CHORUS girl nearest him, opens mouth to speak, thinks better of it and shrugs.)

Exactly, you hadn't an idea in your head. Now you see, if these two dears - (2 CHORUS on her R.) - go that way (Points L.) and we go that way - (Points behind them - then these two darlings - (2 CHORUS L. of KING)

- can go that way, while these two dollies go that way. (Points out front) And then we're bound to get somewhere, aren't we? Right, advance!

(ALL move forward in the directions indicated and, of course, ALL collide in a bunch.)

I don't think that was a very good idea of yours, OSWALD. Obviously, you meant we should all go this way.

(ALL move towards floats and stop just in time with a leg poised over them)

Now think clearly for a moment, Oswald. There's a sheer drop this way, a dead end that way - (Points up stage.) - we've just come that way - (Points R.) - So that's the way to go. Girls lead on! (CHORUS run off L. QUEEN crosses KING and moves L, turning L, turning her head back to talk to KING.) In other words, think what you're doing and look where you're going. (Crashes into L. pros arch) Watch out for that, OSWALD. You might kill yourself on it. (Exit KING and QUEEN L.)

PENNY: (off R) Bonzo! Bonzo! Come back here. (BONZO and PENNY run on R.) Heel, boy, heel. (BONZO puts on a spurt.) Oh very well, elbow, then.

BONZO: (trots sedately to heel)

PENNY: (stopping L) Now look, BONZO, we must find those tarts before anyone else. I know JACK didn't really want to steal them, but ever since I fainted I can't remember where he was told to meet the real culprit, so you must help me BONZO.

BONZO: (thinks then make a "T" with one paw across the other)

PENNY: Tea? He was going to a cafe?

BONZO: (shakes head)

PENNY: Something to do with tea, though.

BONZO: (nods)

PENNY: A tea caddy?

BONZO: (shakes head)

PENNY: A tea pot?

BONZO: (shakes head more firmly)

PENNY: A cup?

BONZO: (shakes head despairingly)

PENNY: A saucer, a spoon?

BONZO: (nods encouragingly)

PENNY: A saucer a spoon? Saucer-a-spoon? - Sorcerers! The Sorcerers's Den! (BONZO shakes her hand, PRINCE and PRINCESS enter R.) Oh, Bravo, Bonzo.

BONZO: (pats himself on back)

PRINCE: Has he found something?

PENNY: Well, sort of. You see, I know who the thief is, only he isn't really. There's another one, who is, even though he didn't actually, whom I don't know but I will soon because Bonzo gave me a valuable clue. He told me where to go.

PRINCESS: I'm not surprised.

PRINCE: What was the clue?

PENNY: "T". We're just off there now.

PRINCE: What, to have tea?

PENNY: No, no, to find the tarts. Only it may be dangerous, we'd better disguise ourselves, Bonzo. Come on.

PRINCE: Well, good luck.

PENNY: Oh, don't worry, we'll find them if it kills us, won't we, Bonzo?

BONZO: (nods and walks slap into pros. arch L.)

PENNY: Steady, Bonzers. I didn't mean it literally. There, I'll kiss it better for you. (Kisses top of head. Turning to others.) You want to watch out for this. (Walks into it herself.) Kiss it better, Bonzo.

(He kisses pros. arch, she shrugs and they exit L.)

PRINCESS: I wonder where they _are_ going?

PRINCE: Well, using my highly superior powers as a detective, I'd say the Sorcerers's Den.

PRINCESS: That's clever. What makes you think that?

PRINCE: Elementary, my dear Watson - I heard Penny say so as we arrived.

PRINCESS: Well, what are we waiting for then?

PRINCE: Well, she also said it might be dangerous.

PRINCESS: Never mind, we can disguise ourselves.

PRINCE: That's a good idea.

PRINCESS: Elementary, my dear Watson.

(QUEEN and KING enter R. side of Auditorium)

QUEEN: Caught you! (HOUSELIGHTS up) Hands up, all of you! Oswald, frisk them to see which one has the tarts.

PRINCESS: I don't think you need bother, Mother. We've an idea where the tarts are - the Sorcerers's Den. We're just off there now.

PRINCE: In disquise.

(They almost walk into pros arch, but manage to avoid it & exit L.)

QUEEN: That's funny - they didn't look in disguise to me. Well, we'd better go there too. (To AUDIENCE.) So sorry to have disturbed you. Oswald got confused. (She moves onto stage. KING shakes his head behind her back then follows her, HOUSE OUT. Close traverse tabs slowly and fly out cloth.) I rather fancy a disguise myself. What shall we go as, Oswald?

KING: (opens mouth)

QUEEN: Of course, obviously. What a quick brain you have, dear. Then, on to the Sorcerer's Den! (She strides R. KING stops her and points L.) What? Oh yes. (Crosses him.) Follow me. (Remembers pros arch.) No, Oswald, *you* lead the way.

KING: (looks rather mystified, but complies and just as he is about to crash, produces a cushion and walks softly into arch)

<u>BLACKOUT</u>

(MUSIC 75. Open traverse tabs.)

2 - 8 - 70

PART 11

SCENE 8 - THE SORCERER'S DEN

(Full set. Cut-out ground-row backing in front of rostrum with opening L.C., behind which is Heath Robinson type space ship. Lights to flash fitted to base. Practical door in space ship, lever on outside beside door. Wing L.& Wing R. Table U.R. with various magical and alchemistic equipment including a magic wand. Large cheval mirror frame R.C.

SORCERERS run on R.)

MERLIN: Wait a minute. There's something wrong.

MERLOUT: Is there? What?

MERLIN: Well, did you hear anything just then?

MERLOUT: No.

MERLIN: That's what's wrong. Back again.

(They go off. EFFECT 11. Loud explosion. They run on.)

That's better.

MERLOUT: What was it, anyway?

MERLIN: Er - let me see. (Consults a notebook.) Experiment nine hundred and fifty.

MERLOUT: Oh, not lead into gold again?

MERLIN: Certainly not. We've just invented Rice Krispies. (Moves to mirror frame.) Well, I must get on with this.

MERLOUT: (poking head through it) What is it, Mr. Merlin?

MERLIN: A mirror frame, my boy. I shall use it to prove that it's all done with mirrors.

MERLOUT: All what is?

MERLIN: I don't know yet. That I shall find out when I've invented mirrors. Oh, by the way, I've finished the space ship to get us to the moon to find the gold. (Moves up to it.)

MERLOUT: It's lovely, Mr. Merlin. Such beautiful lines.

2 - 8 - 71

MERLIN: Thank you, Merlout. Now, whatever you do, don't press this lever (* - like this.

(EFFECT 12. Roar of motors. Lights flash as space ship starts to rise. (If space ship cannot be flown cut between points marked thus - (* - *).)

Aah! Quick, hold it!

(They manage to pull space ship down.)

Whew, that was a near thing.

MERLOUT: Yes. Well, I'll remember that - mustn't press this lever. (Does so.)

(EFFECT 13 roar of motors. Lights flash as space ship rises. They pull it back.)

Why not!

MERLIN: Why not? Why not! Couldn't you see? That's the lever *) that starts it.

(*MERLOUT: Ah, I see. That starts it - when you press it - like this. (Almost presses lever, MERLIN knocks his hand away and leans on lever. EFFECT 14. Roar of motors. Lights flash as space ship starts to rise.)

MERLIN: Aah! Grab it!

(They pull it down *).)

MERLOUT: Does it go bang?

MERLIN: Well, it hasn't yet, but you never know. Nearly everything we do does go with a bang.

(MUSIC 76. THE SORCERERS SONG.)

    First we invented the weasel
    And thought it was the top,
    Because you weaselly make one
    But all it went was pop.

    Next we invented gunpowder,
    But tricky stuff that is,
    Because it turned out to be sherbert
    And all it did was fizz.

> But now our test tubes have got an idea
> That's really very naughty,
> 'Cos each pianissimo we pour in
> Comes out as treble forte!
>
> We work like mad at inventions
> We think we're getting the hang
> But what's the result of our labour?
> It all goes -

(EFFECT 15. Explosion.)

MERLIN: There - we've invented pop numbers!

(They exit R. JACK looks on L.)

JACK: Anybody about? No. Then father can't be here yet. (Hat slips.) It's difficult to tell when it's so dark, though. Oh no, of course. (Pushes hat back. Sees mirror frame. Puts tarts on floor and moves over to frame.) I bet I look like nothing on earth in this. ("Looks" at himself.) Yes, I do. (Turns away and "takes" and turns back.) I really do! I've disappeared. (Runs round to other side of mirror.) I'm not there either! Now, calm down, calm down or you'll only hic! - hic! hic!

(AUDIENCE shout. MUSIC 77. Glass rises.)

Runs down to drink. MERLOUT enters U.R.)

MERLOUT: Where did I leave my Junior Sorcerer's Spell Book? (Searches on table U.R then moves D.R. JACK crosses back to C. MUSIC 78. Glass goes down.)

JACK: Well, thank goodness you're all still there, even if I'm not.

(He and MERLOUT turn simultaneously towards mirror and exhibit identical surprise.)

BOTH: It's me! (Peering closer.) But I don't look quite the same.

MERLOUT: Oh, I need a smaller hat.

JACK: Yes, so do I.

(BOTH turn away, take on the fact that they spoke separately and hurriedly turn back and go through a few experimental motions which are identical reflections of each other. Then turn away.)

MERLOUT: I must get Mr. Merlin to have a look at this. I think he's invented mirrors after all.

(Exit L.)

2 - 8 - 73

JACK: I must put the tarts somewhere safe till father gets here. (Sees space ship.) I wonder what this is? Well, it'll do. (Goes into it.)

(Enter MERLIN R.)

MERLIN: I'm sure Merlout's wrong. I don't remember inventing mirrors. (Moves to mirror as JACK moves out of space ship. They look at each other then both turn away.) I must have done. So that's what a mirror is.

(They turn back.)

BOTH: There's something a bit different about me.

MERLIN: I'm looking younger.

JACK: I'm not - I'm looking older.

(They double take and scratch heads simultaneously then turn away.)

MERLIN: Funnily enough this mirror I've invented works just like that piece of glass I took out. (Exit R. JACK turns back.)

JACK: Oh no, I've gone again. I must pull myself together - (Rushes round to other side of mirror.) If only I could find myself to pull together. (Running through frame.) Come back! (Realises what he has done but checks by putting an arm through frame.) Well, no wonder.

(There is a sound of something being knocked over and a stifled "Ow!" from PENNY off L.)

Perhaps this is father. I'd better hide though to make sure.

(Another stifled "Ow!" off L. JACK goes into space ship and shuts door. PENNY enters cautiously L. disguised as MERLIN, with a rather overlong gown.

PENNY: All clear. Come on, Bonzo.

(BONZO enters disguised as MERLOUT.)

PENNY: Our disguises have worked - jolly good idea, eh Bonzo? Now to find Jack and the tarts. You scout around here while I look through there. (She exits D.R. BONZO freezes as MERLIN and MERLOUT, with a list, enter R.)

MERLIN: Now we'll check the store's list for the space ship. As I call the things out you tick them off.

MERLOUT: Yes, Mr. Merlin. What with?

MERLIN: Really, don't be so helpless, Merlout. Go and invent a pencil.

(Exit MERLOUT R.)

I don't know what these young - (Turning he is confronted by BONZO.) Do try and stay in one place, Merlout.

BONZO: (whines)

MERLIN: Now, don't be silly, you're a big centenarian now. And that reminds me, I've got a bone to pick with you.

BONZO: (nods eagerly and begs)

MERLIN: You've been staying out late at nights. I think you're getting to be a bit of a dog.

BONZO: (not sure how to take this so nods hastily and runs off D.L.)

(PENNY backs on D.R.)

PENNY: Nobody there. (Moves up and comes face to face with MERLIN.)

MERLIN: Now then - (He looks down to mirror frame then back to PENNY.) I ought to be over there to see that.

(They move down to mirror, PENNY to R. and MERLIN to L. PENNY trips on hem of gown just as they get there.)

Hm, my gown must be too long. I'd better cut a bit off. (As he moves away PENNY hastily pulls up gown and JACK cautiously opens door of space ship.) Ah, Merlout, do you know where the scissors are?

JACK: No. (Dodges back into space ship and shuts door.)

MERLOUT: (entering U.R with large pair of prop scissors) Yes.

MERLIN: (swings round in surprise) Well, make up your mind. (Takes scissors.)

(MERLOUT exits R. MERLIN returns to L. of mirror.)

About a couple of inches should do it.   (Sees PENNY'S now very high hem line.)   This is ridiculous.   Now I've got a mini-gown.   Still I must say, I've got a lovely leg for it.

PENNY: Gosh - thanks.

MERLIN: (turn away)   Not at all.

(PENNY realises her mistake and hastily retreats D.R.   MERLIN stops puzzled facing out front.)

I must stop talking to myself.

(PRINCE disguised as MERLIN backs on L.)

PRINCE: (whispering)   You wait there - I'll have a look round.

(MERLIN turns U.S as PRINCE turns in and they confront each other. MERLIN looks down to mirror frame then back to PRINCE and moves back to push frame between them.

MERLIN: I think this mirror's sprung a leak.   Merlout!

(PRINCESS enters L disguised as MERLOUT.)

PRINCESS: Did you mean me, darling?   Oh.

MERLIN: Yes, of course I meant y - (Takes out front.)   Darling!

(PRINCESS backs off L. quickly.)

Merlout, come back here!

MERLOUT: (entering U.R. with large pencil)   Did you call, Mr. Merlin?

MERLIN: Yes, I - (Turns belatedly to him.)   Have you invented roller skates, by any chance?

MERLOUT: No, just this pencil.

MERLIN: Well, check the stores by yourself, then.   I must lie down and try and get away from myself for a bit.   (As he crosses D.R. PENNY enters there.)

I must! (He heads off U.R.   PENNY hastily retreats D.R.)

PRINCE: (calling off L)   Pst!   Quick, change places!   (He exits and PRINCESS takes his place.

2 - 8 - 76

MERLOUT: I'm not sure I've invented this pencil quite right. It might be better with the wood on the outside. What a pity I'm growing up now, I could have invented advertisements and drawn moustaches on them. I wonder how I'd look with a moustache. (Looks in mirror and starts to draw a moustache with pencil. PRINCESS is a little nonplussed but mimes his actions as best she can. MERLOUT cocks head on one side to see effect and seeing none peers closer. Turns away. PRINCESS retreats D.L.) Well, bully for me. I've invented invisible lead. I'd better check those stores though. (He opens space ship door and sees JACK.) No, I needn't bother I'm doing it already. (Realises and slams door shut and leans against it.) I think I'd better lie down too.

(BONZO creeps on D.L. MERLOUT turns and sees him and PRINCESS)

Definitely! (He rushes off U.R.)

BONZO: (indicates that he thinks he is screwy and exits wuff-mumbling to himself D.L.)

(PRINCE enters U.L. PRINCESS turns to him.)

PRINCESS: Hullo. What were you barking for?

PRINCE: Me? I thought it was you. There's something very odd going on here. If we're going to find the tarts we'd better stick together.

(They exit D.R. Enter QUEEN as MERLIN and KING as MERLOUT U.L.)

QUEEN: It's all clear, Oswald. Such an original idea of mine to disquise ourselves as Merlin and Merlout, eh? Now I wonder where the tarts are? Oh, look Oswald, a mirror. Obviously one of those magic mirrors because you can't see anything in it.

(KING steps U.S. of it looking at it.)

        How splendid, at last I can find out.
        "Magic mirror - by the wall,
        Which is the fairest one of all?"

(KING steps to R side of it.)

Oswald? !

(He peers round lower edge of frame.)

Oh, Oswald. Ooh, look out!

(KING runs to L.C. Enter MERLIN R.)

2 - 8 - 77

MERLIN: Well, I feel a bit better now - (Looks in mirror.) But I look worse than ever.

(QUEEN gives a chagrined expression)

Yes, every bit of my five hundred years. (He puts out tongue. QUEEN puts her tongue out rather viciously.) Ugh. I must invent Eno's at once. (Exit U.R.)

QUEEN: That was hardly a very polite reflection.

(JACK opens door of space ship hitting KING who is standing beside it)

KING: Ow!

JACK: Oo! (He slams door.)

QUEEN: Something the matter, dear?

(KING points to space ship and backs away from it to L. as BONZO backs on D.L.)

(turning to U.S. to examine space ship) Oh, what a strange looking thing. (She is about to press it as BONZO and KING collide. KING gives a cry and runs off D.L.)

(turning back) What's the matter, Oswald - Oswald! Whatever's happened to you? Aah! Of course, they've put a spell on you. Oh, what saucy naughterers - naughty sorcerers. (Rushing U.R. searching on table.) What can I do? (Finds a wand.) A magic wand! Dare I?I must! But I can't bear to look, I might make him worse. (With averted head and a hand over her eyes she waves wand at BONZO, who runs off U.L. She turns back.)

Aah! I've made him disappear! I know a magic circle. (She bends over to make circle on ground with wand. KING looks on D.L. is puzzled by her behaviour and moves in to tap her on behind. She looks round fearfully.)

Oswald! Oh, thank goodness. I couldn't have slept in a kennel for the rest of my life.

(They exit D.L. MUSIC 79. ACE puts head on U.L.)

ACE: Aha!

(AUDIENCE shout)

2 - 8 - 78

ACE: Beautiful, beautiful. You're getting a lovely tone quality now as well as the volume. After that nasty bang on the head I gave myself I stopped on the way for a little "thirst-aid". He-he-he! I'm in form tonight. I expect Jack's here by now. (Calling softly.) Jack! Jack! Oh no, of course, he won't answer to Jack while he's disguised as Merlout. (Calling.) Merlout!

MERLOUT: (stepping on U.R. Yes?

JACK: (coming out of space-ship) Yes?

PRINCESS: stepping on D.R. Yes?

(KING steps on D.L. and coughs)

BONZO: (stepping on U.L. Wuff!

(Each is rather put out to see the others)

ACE: Goodness, that fizzy lemonade's strong! I've heard of seeing double, but this is ridiculous.

MERLOUT: Mr. Merlin!

(PENNY and PRINCE enter D.R. MERLIN U.R. and QUEEN D.L., simultaneously)

PENNY:
QUEEN:
PRINCE: Yes?
MERLIN:
ACE:

JACK: Well, which is father? Eeny-meeny -

PENNY: (moving into C.) I say, you rotters have pinched my idea.

QUEEN: (moving in with KING to PENNY'S L.))
No, no, it was our idea, Penny.)
PRINCE &) - Together
PRINCESS: (moving in to PENNY'S R.))
Your idea? It was our idea.)
)

(They continue to argue. MERLIN and MERLOUT move D.R. eyeing them with bewilderment.)

ACE: (breaking D.L.) Beasts, it was my idea first.

MERLOUT: Mr. Merlin, have we invented ourselves lately?

MERLIN: No, I think it must be the time of year - there's a lot of us about.

2 - 8 - 79

QUEEN: But where are the tarts?

(JACK hastily gets inside space ship and shuts door)

PENNY: I've looked everywhere - except in that thing.

MERLIN: That's not a thing. That's our space ship to the moon.

(BONZO yawns and leans on lever, then moves away as it gives under him)

(EFFECT 16. Roar of motors. Lights flash on space ship as it rises. White flash in box set behind space ship. MERLIN and MERLOUT rush up in a vain attempt to stop it and stand peering up. If space ship cannot be flown:- Flash, blackout, roar of motors EFFECT. Strike space ship LIGHTS UP.)

MERLIN: Hm. We must have invented the self starter.

BONZO: (looks over ostentatiously innocent)

QUEEN: Don't just stand there - after it! To the Moon!

PENNY, PRINCE,
& PRINCESS,
MERLIN &
MERLOUT: To the Moon!

(QUEEN, KING, PENNY and BONZO run off L. MERLIN and MERLOUT, PRINCE and PRINCESS off R. ACE moves D.S. Close traverse tabs. Fly in Scene 9 frontcloth if used.)

ACE: (as they go) Yes, to the - wait a minute, how?

(EFFECT 17. Roar of DEMON'S car off L., screech of brakes. DEMON spot up L. DEMON enters D.L.)

DEMON: Just with some simple magic, bash
We'll zoom straight up there, in a flash!

(Flash L. BLACKOUT. Whoosh whistle. EFFECT 18. Loud clonk in flies).

DEMON &
ACE: Ow!

(Lights up. They are sitting on floor rubbing their heads)

ACE: I do not wish to sound aloof
But ev'ry building has a roof.

DEMON: All right, I made a boob - okay.
So - we'll get there another way.
My ultra modern magic kit
Can give my car a quick refit,
And fix a supersonic motor
In the twinkling of a rotor!

(They exit L. FAIRY MUSIC 80. White spot up R. FAIRY breathlessly pedals on R. on her cycle)

FAIRY: Well, lawks-a-mussy-me, my dears,
I'm here at last so calm your fears.
A most unfortunate conjuncture,
I had to stop and mend a puncture.
A tintack made my tube blow out,
A bit of Demon's work, no doubt.
And now, that I may save my face,
I'll have to join this mad moon race;
But I don't feel the least compulsion
To rocketry or jet propulsion;
A more old fashion'd means I'll try -
In other words, I'm going to fly,
'Cos luckily with wings I'm clad.

(Leaps up and falls down on behind.)

Oops! Right back on my launching pad.
Of course, I am a silly chump -
I need to take a <u>running</u> jump!

(MUSIC 81. Runs off R. BLACKOUT. Strike cycle.

2 - 9 - 81

PART 11

SCENE 9 - IN THE AIR

(Open traverse tabs. Cloud cloth and in front of it a cut-out of the basket of a balloon with ropes going up from it. The tail of the balloon can be seen hanging down. (If a frontcloth is not used open tabs to reveal a six-foot flat with cloud backing painted on it and balloon basket set in front of it.) The QUEEN, in a sort of Edwardian motoring type flying costume and BONZO with an old fashioned airman's leather helmet are in basket. BONZO is looking round with a telescope.)

QUEEN: Lovely view up here, isn't it, Bonzo?

BONZO: (nodding) Wuff-wuff.

QUEEN: What a pity there's nothing to see.

BONZO: (looks at AUDIENCE through telescope and jumps up and down barking excitedly)

QUEEN: Careful, Bonzo. You'll upset the basket. What is it, dear?

BONZO: (points to AUDIENCE and hands her telescope)

QUEEN: (looks at AUDIENCE) Ooh yes - a lot of people sitting on a cloud. Let's see if we can get onto a cloud. Throw out the anchor, dear.

BONZO: (finds the anchor attached to a rope. Looks at it a moment then starts to untie it)

QUEEN: (trains telescope onto Orchestra) Oh goody, the Royal Bandmaster's here with the band on a cloud, too. (Turns to BONZO.) Do hurry up and throw that anchor out.

BONZO: (he has finished untying rope and throws anchor offstage)

QUEEN: Wasn't that attached to a rope or anything?

BONZO: (looks at rope he is still holding and hastily puts it behind his back and shakes head)

QUEEN: Never mind, we seem to have stopped anyway. (Climbs out of basket.) Oh, it's a nice firm cloud. I thought it might be like walking on candy floss. Now, I've got a treat for you, Bonzo. I've written a little song all about you. Listen carefully, Bandmaster, and you can pick it up.

(MUSIC 82. "Doggerel Ditty")

>   A bloodhound up in a balloon
>   Is quite a thing to view.
>   He's such an aeronaughty dog -
>   The first of the doggy doggy few!

There, did you like that, Bonzo?

BONZO: (nods enthusiastically)

QUEEN: I tell you what then, we'll let all those people on that big cloud sing it, too. (To AUDIENCE.) Would you like to do that? (Reaction.) I had a suspicion you might. Luckily I've written the words on the balloon. I'll just let a little air out. ("Let's'air out of tail of balloon. Balloon descends with song sheet words printed on it. There. Now, all together. (After a few bars.) No, no. I said all together. Once more. Oh, that was very good wasn't it, Bonzo? What a pity Oswald's not here. He loves singing you know.

(EFFECT 19. Outboard motor. KING enters L. at the front of a broomstick with PENNY seated behind him. Prop outboard motor hanging down at the back of broomstick.)

QUEEN: Oswald!

PENNY: What a bit of luck eh, your Majesty? We found this motorised broomstick in the sorcerers' backyard.

QUEEN: Well, I'm very glad you did. Now you can sing this little song with us and all the people on that big cloud.

(KING nods enthusiastically, then had an idea, points to AUDIENCE then to stage and indicates small people.)

Oh yes, Oswald, what a spiffing notion! He suggests we get some of the children to come up onto our cloud to sing. Isn't that clever? So original too. Penny, you direct the traffic flow, dear.

(Houselights up.)

Ah, how fortunate. The sun's come out from behind our cloud.

(ALL help the children onto stage. Ad lib and return them to their seats. Houselights out.)

Now, just once more and then we must be getting on with our journey. Everybody this time and as loud as you can.

(As song is sung for last time KING and PENNY exit R. on broomstick. QUEEN and BONZO get back into basket. Tabs close. MUSIC 83. Lights fade. Bring up FAIRY spot R. FAIRY enters R. with large "Milky Way" bar.)

FAIRY: I'm back my dears and - Oh, I say,
Do please excuse this Milky Way,
I found it floating in the sky.
I really did. I can't think why.
I'm back, my dears, because I find
Both Prince and Princess left behind.
Don't worry though, I'll get them there,
For exercise and good fresh air
Have seen that I the strength don't lack
To fly them double pig-a-back.

(As she exits R.- BLACKOUT.)

(MUSIC 84. Open traverse tabs.)

2 -10- 84

PART 11

SCENE 10 - ON THE MOON

(Full set. Cut-out ground row of bluish moonscape along back of rostrum Shattered remains of space ship having apparently landed nose first in C. on rostrum concealing sword and dagger. Wing L. and wing R. Large gold cross on wing R. beneath it several large prop gold rocks. Seat-like broken off stalagmite D. R. C. Pedestal like stalagmite U. L. C.

EFFECT 20. In Blackout Whooshy music ends in loud crash. Lights half up to reveal JACK in the middle of space ship wreckage on his back kicking his legs in the air. He lets them fall to the ground and sits up. He still holds dish of tarts)

JACK: I think I've arrived. (Feels himself tenderly as he rises.) No bones broken either. Even the tarts are all right, except for the two that fell out on the way, and the went into orbit. (Puts tarts on pedestal stalagmite U. L. C.) It's rather dark here, isn't it? If this is the moon why isn't there any moonlight?

(Lights come up as a huge earth rises on cyc O. P. Various countries are quite visible on it and are clearly marked with their names except that Africa has England written on it.)

Ah, that's better. (Looks round and sees Earth.) Oh, of course, the Earth's rising. There, I always said that was England when I was at school and they told me I was wrong. It's a lovely full earth tonight, isn't it? Perhaps it's a harvest earth. "Shine on, shine on, Harvest Earth
    For all your worth,
    I ain't had no loving since January,
    February, June and "
Rotten place for song writers this. Still, I don't suppose there are any. There may be some local inhabitants, though. I wonder what I should say to them? "How"!? Oh no, of course - "Take me to your leader". (Moving L.) That is if I see any. (Evidently sees something off L.) Waah! (He turns and runs off R.)

(MUSIC 85. Enter the MOON MONSTER L. He has a shaggy beard and mane, two short arms in front, six humps, fourteen legs, with a pair of wings by No. 3 legs (in directions each pair is numbered 1 - 7 from front to back.) He also has a tail and wears a mini-kilt with a sporran.)

MOON MONSTER: Och, look at that now, another Earth rocket's landed. You can't get a bit of peace on the moon these days. (Lifting Downstage legs and shaking feet.) I've been running round half the day dodging all the things flying round here now and my feet are killing me. I must take the weight off them a bit. (No. 7 legs sink sharply onto stalagmite seat and rise again.) Ooh! I forgo that nasty jab I got from a moon probe the other day.

2 -10- 85

(No. 7 legs lower themselves more gently onto seat then 6 sits on 7, 5 on 6 etc.) Ah, that's better. Och, there's nothing like a good scratch. Of course, I haven't always lived on the moon. No, I used to live on Earth, in a place called Loch Ness. I was very happy there, but after a while every time I took a bath in the loch people peered at me with binoculars and tried to photograph me. I had to give up bathing altogether and make do with a good wash-down in a basin - but it's very awkward for me standing in a basin. So I flew up here. And now the whole thing's happening again, only worse - they're sending artificial satellites with television cameras. Well, would you like it every time you had a bath they showed you on the telly? (Rises.) I think I'll move to Mars, they've got some lovely canals for bathing in there. All I ask for is a little bit of privacy.

(MUSIC 86. "Monster's Song".)

> I want to be just left alone,
> Somewhere entirely on my own,
> Me and my shaggy beard and mane, two short arms in
>   front, six humps, fourteen legs with a pair of wings
>   by No. 3 legs and a tail.
>
> Give me a comfy old settee,
> Twenty nine yards by five foot three,
> For me and my shaggy beard, etc.
>
> Then in the long winter evenings
> I will go to my easy chair,
> And there I'll sit and count myself
> To see if I'm all there.
>
> P'raps some day love may come my way,
> Someone who'll look at me and say -
> That she's also got a shaggy beard, etc.

(During number he does a sort of Tiller Girl dance routine in which after a while No. 4 legs are always at variance with the others, and he ends up in a complete circle facing his own behind.)

That's not right. (He straightens himself out till he is in a line facing L., but No. 4 legs in process move D.S. and turn about to face R. and Nos. 5 and 3 are close up to each other.) Nor's that. Now let's all of me face the same way. (No. 2 legs move down out of line with feet facing front. No. 1 and 3 remain facing L. No. 4 moves into line but with feet pointing U.S. No. 5 comes down at an angle to No. 4 with feet pointing R. No. 7 closes up to No. 6 with feet pointing L.) I'm just a crazy-mixed up monster. (Sniffs.) Ooh, what's that I can smell? Jam tarts! (All the feet hastily re-arrange themselves so that the MONSTER is in line facing L. His tail wags. He sniffs again.) No, I can't believe it. I used to love jam tarts when I was on earth, but there's only green cheese to eat here. It grows like a sort of grass. You cut it and you've got cheese straws. (Sniffs, tail wagging.) Yes, I'm sure it's jam tarts. (Sees them.) It is! Och, I'll have a lovely feast.

(As he moves towards tarts EFFECT 21. Outboard motor.)

MONSTER: What's that? Don't tell me they're landing men now. I just shrink from people, you know. (All legs close up tight behind each other.) You see - I've shrunk. (Starts moving off L.)

(EFFECT 22. Motor backfires (Pistol Shot.) MONSTER runs off. Enter R. KING, PENNY, BONZO and QUEEN on broomstick, backfiring continues. ALL jump each time particularly the QUEEN who is on the end.

PENNY: Well done, sire, a three point landing.

(QUEEN falls off end as broomstick stops in C.)

QUEEN: A four point dear. Still at least it's nice to be sitting on something that doesn't go bang all the time. I think that broomstick's on it's last twigs. Such a pity Oswald rammed and burst the balloon. The basket was much more comfortable, wasn't it, Bonzo?

BONZO: (nodding & dismounting) Wuff-wuff.

PENNY: (patting him) Oh well, he's used to baskets.

QUEEN: Strangely enough I'm not, but a basket seemed more me somehow.

(KING nods & opens mouth.)

QUEEN: Oswald! Anyway, at least you seem to be able to control that thing now.

(EFFECT 23. Burst of noise from outboard motor & Broomstick apparently suddenly shoots away with KING off D.L. OTHERS run in a group to L.)

QUEEN: Oswald, come back, come back! Oswald!

(ALL jump back as he hurtles on D.L. and straight across to go off D.R.)

He's gone! Oh, Oswald.

PENNY: It's all right, your Majesty, he'll be back, won't he, Bonzo?

BONZO: (shakes head.)

PENNY: (urgently aside) The other yes, Bonzo.

BONZO: (contritely nods head)

PENNY: There you see.

QUEEN: No, no he's gone for good. How can he possibly drive without me sitting at the back telling him what to do? I shall never see him again. Never again hear the dear nod of his head, never again feel the gentle touch of his -

(KING shoots on D. L. and enters tentatively and quietly above them. They move into a line D. C. KING on L. QUEEN next then PENNY then BONZO. KING opens mouth.)

Yes, I know dear, you just got carried away. But I do feel we should all stick together, don't you, Penny?

PENNY: Rather, I mean this is a strange planet. We don't know what else there may be here.

QUEEN: Probably nothing. Can you see anything, Oswald?

KING: (turns to look L. encountering MONSTER'S face. Turns back to the QUEEN and shakes head. Does a delayed take on the MONSTER then runs off D. L. silently shouting "help". MONSTER looks puzzled and moves behind them)

QUEEN: Oswald can't see anything.

PENNY: Can you see anything, Bonzo?

BONZO: (lifts an ear with a forepaw and shakes head)

PENNY: Oh, Bonzo. All right, can you hear anything.

(BONZO puts a forepaw to eyes and scans R. then shakes head. MONSTER moves to R. of him and BONZO turns shake into a nod as he registers MONSTER and runs off D. R.)

PENNY: It's difficult to tell with Bonzo but I think he said no.

QUEEN: Oh good. (Turning to L.) Now Oswald - Oswald's gone again. Is Bonzo there?

PENNY: Yes, of cour - oooher... (Turning to BONZO she encounters MONSTER and faints into QUEEN'S arms, while MONSTER hastily retreats upstage.)

QUEEN: Gracious, what can have come over the child? (Lays her against stalagmite D. R. C.)

MONSTER: I think she's fainted.

QUEEN: Well, of course, she's - that's very odd. I heard a voice. (To AUDIENCE.) I say, is there anyone here? (AUDIENCE shout.) Who is it? (Shout.) A Monster! Oh, how dreadful. Where is it? (Shout.) Behind me? I can hardly bring myself to look.

(QUEEN turns to L. very slowly to look U.S. MONSTER closes up onto its front so none of it is directly behind her. She turns to face front quickly and MONSTER spreads itself out again.)

QUEEN: It's not. (Shout.) Well, I'll look again. I'll look all round. (She walks round in a large circle with the MONSTER following behind her.) I can't see a monster. (Shout.) It must be a very small monster then. (Shout.) Oh, yes, it is (Shout.) Oh yes, it is, etc.

MONSTER: (moving down to her R.) Oh no, I'm not.

QUEEN: (turning to MONSTER) Oh yes, you are. Aaah! (Turns and runs off L.)

MONSTER: (moving round into a line facing L.) That's what I don't like about people - they're so hysterical. Well, now I can eat those jam tarts, anyway.

(JACK enters D.R.)

JACK: Not a soul in - (Comes face to rear with MONSTER'S behind.) Ooh. A local. Take me to your leader.

(MONSTER'S tail wags and No. 7 D.S. leg points forward.)

Ta. (Moves to MONSTER'S head.) Are you the - Oh dear, hic - hic - hic!

(AUDIENCE shout. MUSIC 87. Glass shoots up. He runs and drinks.)

MONSTER: That's funny, he speaks Latin.

JACK: (returning to head of MONSTER) That's better. (MUSIC 88. Glass descends.) Thank goodness there's water on the moon.

MONSTER: Hic.

JACK: Hic?

MONSTER: Hic, haec, hoc.

JACK: Are you taking the hickey - I mean the Mickey?

MONSTER: Oh, you do speak English like the rest of them.

JACK: Do you mean there are some others here?

MONSTER: Aye, there's one of them over there.

JACK: (turns and sees PENNY) Penny! (Rushes to her and tries to revive her.) Penny! It's me, Jack.

PENNY: D.L.)	(sitting up) Jack? Jack! (Sees MONSTER.) Aah! (Runs off
JACK:	I see it all now. You're a dragon and you go round kidnapping maidens.
MONSTER:	Oh dear, your name's not George, is it?
JACK:	No, Jack.
MONSTER:	Ah, I'm all right then. You won't want to fight me.
JACK:	Certainly I will you fiend - in - in - fiendish form. (Putting up fists and makes a feint towards MONSTER.)
MONSTER:	Now, don't do that, don't do that.
JACK:	Why not?
MONSTER:	'Cos I'm very easily frightened and I'll run away.
JACK:	Well, I'm not and I won't.

(EFFECT 24. Lound explosion off. JACK and MONSTER scream. JACK runs off D.L. MONSTER L. The wail of voices getting nearer and nearer off R. SORCERERS leap on stage each holding the stick of a burnt out fire work rocket and land in a thudding heap. They are wearing space helmets and very loose combinations.)

MERLIN: Well, well. I never thought we'd become Flying Sorcerers. It makes excellent rocket fuel that self-raising flour we invented.

MERLOUT: Perhaps we ought to invent November the fifth too. We could make a lot of money out of it.

MERLIN: A very good idea. Remind me when we get back. By the way, I did tell you to bring some of the flour with you, didn't I?

MERLOUT: No.

MERLIN: Oh. Don't bother to remind me then. We shan't be going back. What a bit of luck I invented these space suits.

MERLOUT: (looking at them dubiously) Are you sure they're space suits, Mr. Merlin?

MERLIN: Of course. There's plenty of space in them, anyway. We've landed right on target. (Takes out map.) There's the gold cross and this must be the gold we came to find. (Picks up a rock, it is marked 22 ct.) Yes, twenty-two carats. Look. (Turns it over to show a number of carrots imbedded in it.)

2-10-90

MERLOUT: Has it got jam tarts marked on the map?

MERLIN: (scanning map) No.

MERLOUT: It ought to have, there are some here.

MERLIN: Really: I'll put them in then. (Marking map.) Jam Tarts here. On second thoughts, I won't bother. Let's eat them.

MERLOUT: Yes.

JACK: (running on D. L.) Hey, don't eat those, they're mine. (Takes them.) Well, sort of.

(QUEEN enters L. followed by KING.)

QUEEN: Ah, Jack - Oswald, the Jam Tarts!

PENNY: (running on D. L.) The tarts?

BONZO: (running on D. R. Wuff-wuff?

MERLIN: I'd no idea the moon was so densely populated.

QUEEN: Jack, don't tell me it was you who stole them?

JACK: Yes, in a way, but I didn't want to really. I only did it because - well, anyway I promise I won't again.

QUEEN: Oh, Jack, I'm at a loss for words.

KING: Really? Then leave this to me, Henrietta. (Rolling up sleeves.) I will deal with the situation.

QUEEN: What's come over you, Oswald? You only speak once in a blue moon.

KING: Well, we're in a blue moon, aren't we? And if he hadn't stolen the tarts we shouldn't be. Jack, you deserve a thorough spanking for all the trouble you've caused. Because of you I've had to dress up as a sorcerer, cavort about on a broomstick, and dodge moon monsters. And what has been the result of it all?

QUEEN: Isn't he lovely when he gets going?

KING: Be quiet, Henrietta. The result has been that I've enjoyed every minute of it. I lead a very dull life and I can't thank you enough. Therefore - bend down.

(JACK bends over. KING taps him lightly.)

There that's dealt with that. We obviously shan't get back to earth with these, so who's for a jam tart?

(MONSTER runs in L. and snatches plate. All cower to R. (Only legs 1 - 3 should be onstage))

MONSTER: Me! And I'm afraid I'm going to be a pig and eat them all.

(White flash R. MUSIC 89. FAIRY leaps on U.R. on rostrum.)

FAIRY: Oh no, you won't!

(As MONSTER blinks at her she moves down and takes tarts from him.)

FAIRY: Without them see,
There can't no happy ending be.
(Recovers her breath a little, patting MONSTER.)
    I didn't mean to sound so rough,
    It's just that I'm all out of puff.
    From earth to here is quite a hop,
    specially carrying two on top.
    For hence the Royal pair I've flown
    To claim each other for their own.

(Enter PRINCE and PRINCESS on rostrum.)

    See here they come now, hand in hand
    To eat the tarts at last as plann'd.

(As she hands tarts to PRINCE EFFECT 25, roar of DEMON'S car, screech of brakes and bonk. MONSTER closes up on itself, other legs surging on stage as if hit.)

MONSTER: Ouch! Now what's that arriving here?
Something's biffed me in the rear.

(Green flash L. as DEMON leaps on L. followed by ACE.)

DEMON: Relax, it's just a hold-up, folks. (Snatches tarts and gives them to ACE.)

QUEEN: Ace! What's the meaning of this hoax?

ACE: To put it very simply, Ma'am,
That with the tarts we're going to scram!

(Turns to run off L. PENNY grabs tarts and runs R. DEMON moves down and intercepts, PRINCE whisks them off DEMON and passes them to PRINCESS who passes them to QUEEN who passes them to MERLOUT who doesn't take them.)

MERLOUT: No thanks, I'm not hungry.

ACE: (taking them) I am.

(BONZO moves in and takes them.)

PENNY: Well done, Bonzo! To me!

(BONZO looks at her but unfortunately throws them to DEMON who gives them to ACE who dashes over catwalk into auditorium. Houselights up. MUSIC 90. The Auditorium directions are given from the point of view of the audience.

The following business was designed for an auditorium with aisles along either side joined by a transverse aisle about half-way along; in other words, the aisles are in the shape of an "H". The entrances to the auditorium are at the back L. and R. and at the L. and R. sides on a level with the transverse aisle. A passage leads from a stage pass door to the entrance at R. of auditorium and other passages connect all the other entrances. Obviously the business will have to be rearranged to suit the auditorium in which it is performed. In doing so, note that in the script the focus of interest is continually switched back and forth between the stage and auditorium and this is the effect that should be striven for.

ACE streaks up R. hand aisle to exit at R. back.)

QUEEN: After him!

(PENNY, JACK, PRINCE and PRINCESS, BONZO, KING and QUEEN run into auditorium following ACE. MERLIN, MERLOUT and FAIRY move down to floats. DEMON sneaks off L. during this. JACK and PENNY, PRINCE and PRINCESS re-enter at L. back.)

JACK: Where is he?

(DEMON runs on L. with duplicate plate of tarts.)

DEMON: Aha!

PENNY: He's got them!

(JACK, PENNY, PRINCE and PRINCESS run down L. aisle, across transverse aisle towards catwalk, while onstage MONSTER grabs tarts from DEMON. FAIRY takes them from MONSTER and runs off R. with them.)

DEMON: Now, look what you've done you overgrown centipede!

(ACE appears (with original set of tarts) at L. side entrance of auditorium and makes across transverse aisle.)

ACE: All right, I've got them!

(DEMON runs off L. ACE is making for exit at R. side of auditorium but there encounters KING, QUEEN and BONZO. JACK, PENNY, PRINCE and PRINCESS have moved up from catwalk towards him, he turns and runs up R. aisle and out at R. back with them. They follow, but before they reach exit DEMON appears at R. side of auditorium with third plate of tarts. FAIRY runs off R.

DEMON: I've got them!

(He runs off at L. side of auditorium. ALL run in pursuit down R. aisle and across transverse. PRINCE and PRINCESS drop off to exit at R. side entrance, FAIRY runs on R. onstage with 2nd plate of tarts.)

FAIRY: Now, I have.

(MONSTER takes them from her.)

MONSTER: Now me.

(MERLIN and MERLOUT take them from MONSTER.)

SORCERERS: Now us! (They run off L. ACE runs on at R. of Auditorium with original plate.)

ACE: Now me again.

(Runs towards catwalk to be met by FAIRY coming down towards him. Others are returning across transverse aisle. He runs up R. aisle and exits at back. All follow him out including FAIRY, DEMON runs on at L. side with his plate of tarts and across transverse aisle. He meets SORCERERS at L. side entrance.

DEMON: I went that way. (Points towards catwalk.)

SORCERERS: Thanks.

(They run towards catwalk. DEMON runs off at R. side. SORCERERS register, stop and run back. They listen.

MERLOUT: I can hear him coming.

MERLIN: We'll pounce on him.

(They wait either side of entrance. QUEEN appears. They grab her.)

BOTH: Got you! Oh sorry.

(BONZO runs in at L. side of auditorium. PENNY at L. back.)

BONZO: (pointing vigorously the way he has come) Wuff-wuff-wuff-wuff-wuff.

PENNY: All right, Bonzo, we'll get him. Pounce.

(They pounce on JACK who comes in at L. side.)

Oh, sorry, Jack.

2 - 10 - 94

(PRINCESS runs on L. onstage.)

PRINCESS: Have you got them?

(FAIRY runs in at R. back and KING at L. back of auditorium.)

FAIRY: Where are they?

(DEMON runs on D. L. onstage.)

ALL: (in Auditorium) After him! (They run towards stage, some getting onto steps of catwalk.)

DEMON: I haven't got them.

(ACE runs on L.)

ALL: (in Auditorium) He's got them.

ACE: I haven't.

ALL: (in Auditorium) Then who's got the tarts?

(PRINCE enters U. R. on rostrum with 4th plate of tarts.)

PRINCE: I have!

OTHERS: (coming on stage) Hooray!

(HOUSE OUT)

ACE and DEMON: He won't for long.

(They draw swords. MUSIC 91. They move menacingly towards others who hurry to sides of stage. ACE and DEMON turn to advance slowly on PRINCE.)

FAIRY: Now, now that's coming it too strong.

Two onto one! I'll cast a spell,
At least he shall be armed as well.

(Waves wand. Flash U. C. under cover of which PRINCE takes sword and dagger from behind space ship on rostrum, and puts dish of tarts down on rostrum. Fight ensues in which PRINCE is victorious over both opponents, disarming the DEMON and pinning the ACE over the staligmite R. C.)

ACE: I yield.

OTHERS: Hip, Hip.

2 - 10 - 95

DEMON: Aw, save the hips,
I know when I have had my chips.

(DEMON stamps off L. EFFECT 26. We hear his car roar off.)

FAIRY: And so to join Diamonds and Hearts
I prithee eat of these jam tarts.

(reveals plate to show it is empty. General gasp. MONSTER has been unobtrusively eating them during fight.)

MONSTER: (still with mouth rather full)

Och, dear, my appetite's just vicious.
Believe me though, they were delicious.

FAIRY: You greedy thing! Now by your plunder,
You've torn two loving hearts asunder.

JACK: Here wait a jiff, two tarts fell out
And are in orbit round about.

FAIRY: Then I can swiftly cease their flight
And thus at last all wrongs put right.

(FAIRY waves wand. Whizz whistle. Two jam tarts fly on L. and R. and are caught by KING and QUEEN.)

QUEEN: Neatly wrapped in polythene, too. (Giving one to PRINCE.)
There one for you.

KING: (giving one to PRINCESS) And one for you.

PRINCE and   With the kiss I thus impart
PRINCESS: (Each kisses tart.)
             I pledge thee all my love, my heart,
             (Each holds tart for the other to bite.)

KING and
QUEEN: Aah!

FAIRY: And while we're here, I understand
Another romance needs a hand
'Tis for this pair I make so bold

(Indicates JACK and PENNY with wand.)

ACE: Then my consent, I'll not withold.

BONZO: Wuff-wuff. (Gives PENNY a smacking dog kiss. Points to PENNY then gives her hand to JACK and points to himself.)

2 - 10 - 96

PENNY: Oh, rather, Bonzo.

JACK: What's he say?

PRINCESS: Why, that he'll give the bride away.

BONZO: (nods)

FAIRY: Now back to earth then with all speed.
A flying charabanc 'twill need
To give so many safe descent
But first, I must the thing invent.

(Exit R.)

MERLOUT: A charabanc? That sounds like us
What sort of bang is that?

MERLIN: A bus. I have invented something, though.

(ALL put hands to ears.)

OTHERS: What is it? Is it noisy?

MERLIN: No. (Producing and giving out music sheets.)
A song to celebrate this story
Arranged for soloists
(giving music to MONSTER) and chori.

(MUSIC 92. "Queen of Hearts" Handelian number.

ALL: The Queen of Hearts she made some tarts
The Queen of Hearts she made some tarts,
All on a Summer's day,
All on a Summer's day.
The Knave of Hearts he stole those tarts
And took them clean away
And took them, took them, took them, took them,
   took them, took them, took them, took them,
Clean away.

The King of Hearts called for those tarts
And beat the Knave full sore
And beat the Knave
And beat the Knave
And beat the Knave full sore, full sore, full sore.

The Knave of Hearts brought back those tarts
And vowed he'd steal no more.
The Knave of Hearts brought back those tarts
And vowed he'd steal no more.
And vowed he'd steal no more, no more, no more.
And vowed he'd steal no more.

BLACKOUT. Close traverse tabs.

2 - 11 - 97

PART 11
SCENE 11 - DOWN TO EARTH

(Tabs. Enter FAIRY R. humming wedding march.)

FAIRY: Most satisfactory, I must say;
Old-fashioned means have won the day,
The Demon's power's void and null -
Which, truth to tell's a trifle dull.
I dearly love a bit of strife -
It gives that extra zip to life!

(Enter DEMON dejectedly L.)

Ah, Demon. Where's the usual din?

DEMON: All right, you've won, don't rub it in,
You've heard the last of my poor car -
I ran into a shooting star.
You've heard the last of me as well;
My number down the charts has fell
Till now I'm "Number One Dead Wire".
There's nothing left but to retire.

FAIRY: And you so young. It seems a shame.
(sighs) Without you things won't seem the same.
Don't let one setback put you off,
Just try - although I know you'll scoff -
A more old-fashioned sort of line.

DEMON: What - all that "thee" and "thou" and "thine"?
And that "Ten thousand curses" stuff,
With gnashing teeth and accents gruff?
In fact, the heavy-acting bit?

FAIRY: Why, yes, that is exactly it.
And though for you to win's taboo,
You'll find it's much more fun to do!

(MUSIC 93. "Swing"   Reprise)

FAIRY: You gotta be gentle, you gotta have poise,
You mustn't make a really noisy noise;
You need deportment and dignity
For example - look at me -
(trips over wand)
You gotta have manners and be polaite
You gotta have charm to Demon-strate.
If you can do this little thing
Then you will really start to swing.

2 - 12 - 98

DEMON: Me a shy retiring creature?
That's a laugh right off the chest.
O.K., baby, you're the teacher,
I will do my little best.
I will smile a little slicker,
Light and sweetness will I bring
I will emulate the Vicar,
Then perhaps I'll really swing.

(At the end of number as they exit L. and R. open traverse tabs for Scene 12.)

2 - 12 - 99

PART 11

SCENE 12 - THE GRAND WEDDING RECEPTION
AT THE HOUSE OF CARDS

(Full set. Palace decor, preferably with card motif. Cut-out ground row along back of rostrum. Steps down in C. of rostrum. Palace wings L. and R.

MUSIC 94. CHORUS enter L. and R. on rostrum for walkdown. Each pair meets in C. of rostrum and comes D.C. to take their bow. They then split and back away to form diagonal lines L. and R. The principals follow a similar procedure, forming diagonal lines in front of CHORUS. FAIRY enter from R. and DEMON L. to R. and L: MOON MONSTER from L. to L; BONZO from R.to R ; ACE L. to L; KING L. to L: QUEEN R. to R. MUSIC 95. ALL turn in as PRINCE enters R. and PRINCESS L. and meet in C of rostrum.)

ALL: Hurray!

(They move down C. to take their bow. Principals move into line with them. CHORUS move up onto rostrum.)

PRINCE: And thus our simple story's told.

PRINCESS: We have found love.

QUEEN: The tarts

SORCERERS: And gold.

QUEEN: And Oswald won't get tummy ache
'Cos I again need never bake.
The Ace has promis'd to behave
And to be guided by the Knave.

ACE: Or rather by my in-law'd daughter.

JACK: So now - three cheers! Hic.

ALL: (encouraging AUDIENCE) Hiccup water!

(MUSIC 96. Glass rises, KNAVE rushes and drinks. MUSIC 97. Glass descends.)

JACK: Thanks and p'raps you'd very kindly, too,
Just give old dad a last -

ALL: (encouraging AUDIENCE) Hiss, boo!

QUEEN: And lastly, as is only right,
I'll say the final word - (Takes breath.)

KING: Good night!

(MUSIC 98. Reprise.)

> It's over; you've had it; it's ended.
> We have had a really lovely time
> Playing in our Pantomime;
> We'll be very sorry when the last curtain has descended.
> So here's our last chance to address you.
> Ere we go upon our homeward way,
> Let us blow a kiss to you and say,
> "Good evening,
> Good journey,
> God bless you!"

<u>CURTAIN</u>

PROPERTY AND FURNITURE PLOT

SET ON STAGE THROUGHOUT.

In front of pros arch R: Small cut-out well, without bucket or rope Fitted with water squirt to be operated off. A plastic tumbler, with straws, on a nylon line to raise and lower it operated off.

PART 1
SCENE 1

Set on Stage: In front of Sorcerers's wing L: trick door mat fitted with nylon line to pull it off L.
On wing: window-box with flowers concealed inside it on nylon lines to pull them up from offstage.
Under window-box: large bed spring and large prop dog bone.

Off R.

Large prop dog bone	PENNY
Truncheon	BONZO
Sedan Chair	KING and QUEEN

(This has a curtained window at sides and front with a royal coat of arms painted below window on D.S. side. It can be simply constructed on a frame about 2 ft. square of 2" x 2", with the ceiling, back, half-front and half-sides of hardboard. Inside there should be a narrow plank seat and a floor strut on which to rest the feet.)

Piggy bank containing one coin, small torch	KING
Satchel containing song sheets	PRINCE
Police handbook	PRINCESS

Off L.

Police scooter	PRINCESS

(This can be a child's scooter mocked-up)

Magazine."THE SCOUNDREL" with huge prop club projecting from it	JACK
Divining rod	BONZO
Dustbin labelled "FAILED EXPERIMENTS"	MERLOUT

A mess labelled "EXPERIMENT 904", trick wand (to turn into bunch of flowers).	MERLIN
Head bandage, sling and cushion to tie on	ACE
4 shopping baskets, (3 containing groceries)	RUMMY
Foot bandage	ACE
Map showing a large square labelled "MOON" on all four sides with gold cross exactly in the middle	MERLIN
Second foot bandage	ACE

Personal

PENNY: Whistle without pea, notebook and pencil

SCENE 2

Off R.

Fairy cycle with bell	FAIRY

Personal

FAIRY   Wand

SCENE 3

Set on stage   Detachable tap on backing

Table R.C. with ping pong ball and cotton wool balls on it

Trick stove L.C. to fall into pieces. 2 frying pans on stove. (Stove requires a solid base about 3'6" x 1'6" mounted on four short legs. The lamp to glow red is attached to the base. The front and sides of the stove are painted gauze on 2" x 1" frames, the back hardboard on a similar frame firmly attached to the base. The front and sides are placed on the base and pin-hinged together and to the back. The pins of the pin hinges are stapled to the stove top, which should also be of hardboard on a wooden frame. There are two nylon lines attached to the top. These are pulled from offstage to lift the top when the explosion occurs thus releasing the pin hinges. Nylon lines are also attached to the sides and are pulled at the same time to make them fall away leaving the front to fall of its own accord.)

Off R.

Apron, feather duster and shooting stick	RUMMY
Large mixing bowl	KING
Large garden sieve	JACK
Tray with tart pans	PENNY
Jug and large wooden spoon	BONZO
Large prop rolling pin	QUEEN
Dog bone	BONZO

Off L.

Phial	DEMON
Large trick bag of flour. (bag over framework to make it appear full, leaving cavity to take butter and salt packets)	
Large packet of butter	CHORUS
Large packet of salt	
Jars of plum, strawberry, blackcurrant, apricot, greengage jam and lemon curd and mincemeat. Wooden spoons in jars	
Large box of "RENNIES"	RUMMY
Tattered remains of flour bag	MERLOUT
Duplicate of trick bag containing pastry dough. (A gluten dough such as is used to make starch-reduced breads is most suitable for the stretching business. This can be stored in a covered tin containing a saline solution.	KING
Charred tarts	To be thrown on.

SCENE 4.

Off L.

Picture frame	ACE
Large box labelled "INSTANT VILLAIN'S KIT" containing : cosh, brick, jemmies, packets of moustaches, fibs, disguises, dastardly schemes, curses and forgery nibs. Large balloon	To be slid on

4.

SCENE 5

Set on Stage   In Doll's House truck R: Stove with large plate of tarts in oven. Small table with cook's hat and pastry making utensils on it.

On plum tree L: detachable plums

By wing L: Wooden bucket

In salt mine U. C: Packet of Cerebos salt

On trick wheat R: Detachable ears

Off as desired

Bag of wheat seed	1st CHORUS FAIRY
Plum stone	3rd CHORUS FAIRY
Wooden bucket and milking stool	4th CHORUS FAIRY
Churn containing packet marked "BUTTER"	5th CHORUS FAIRY
Small pick	6th CHORUS FAIRY

Off L.

Packet of flour   To come out of mill

PART 11
SCENE 6

Off R.

Plate of tarts   BONZO

Off L.

Staff   RUMMY

Long black cloak, black hat, black mask.
Practical water pistol   ACE

Personal

CHORUS: Reticules containing Policewomen's caps, Truncheon

PENNY: Truncheon

SCENE 7

Off R.

Cushion   KING

CHECK JACK has tarts to make entrance R.

SCENE 8

Set on Stage: Table U.R. with various magical and alchemistic
                equipment including a magic wand.
                R.C. Large cheval mirror frame on stand.

Off R.

Stores list   MERLOUT

Large prop scissors   MERLOUT

Large pencil   MERLOUT

Fairy cycle   FAIRY

Off L.

CHECK JACK has plate of tarts

Personal

MERLIN: Notebook

SCENE 9

Set on Stage: Telescope in balloon basket. Anchor on rope to
                balloon basket.

Off R.

Large prop "MILKY WAY" bar.   FAIRY

Off L.

Broomstick with prop outboard motor at rear.   KING and PENNY

SCENE 10

Set on Stage   By wing R: Large prop gold rocks. One marked
                "22 ct." on one side, a number of carrots imbedded
                in the other.
                Behind space ship remains on rostrum: sword and
                dagger.
                CHECK JACK has plate of tarts to begin.

Off R.

Motorized broomstick	KING, QUEEN, BONZO and PENNY
Music sheets, Moon Map	MERLIN
2 burnt out firework rockets	SORCERERS
4th plate of tarts	PRINCE

Off L.

2nd plate of tarts	DEMON
2 swords	ACE and DEMON

Off R. in Auditorium

3rd plate of tarts	DEMON

MUSIC PLOT

PART 1

1. Overture

SCENE 1.

2.	Opening Chorus, "IT'S SUMMER"	CHORUS
3.	Penny's entrance music	Orchestra
4.	Princess's entrance music	Orchestra
5.	"THE MAN FOR ME"	PRINCESS & CHORUS
6.	Ace's entrance music	Orchestra
7.	Reprise 6	"
8.	Jack's entrance music	"
9.	Reprise 6	"
10.	Bonzo's entrance music	"
11.	Glass rising music	"
12.	Glass descending music	"
13.	Reprise 11	"

14.	Reprise 12	Orchestra
15.	Reprise 11	"
16.	Reprise 12	"
17.	Reprise 11	"
18.	Reprise 12	"
19.	Glass half rising music	"
20.	Glass shooting up music	"
21.	Reprise 12	"
22.	Reprise 11	"
23.	Reprise 12	"
24.	"THE CHOPPING SONG"	JACK and PENNY
25.	Reprise 6	Orchestra
26.	Fanfare	"
27.	Sorcerers' music	"
28.	"SONG OF SIXPENCE"	KING and QUEEN
29.	Reprise 6	Orchestra
30.	"SONGS FOR SALE"	PRINCE and CHORUS
31.	"EVERYTHING IS DIFFERENT"	PRINCE & PRINCESS
32.	Reprise 6	Orchestra
33.	" 27	"
34.	" 6	"
35.	" 26	"
36.	" 26	"
37.	"IT'S SUMMER", reprise 2	Ensemble

(Continue, orchestra only, as link to next scene)

SCENE 2.

38.	Fairy Music	Orchestra
39.	Demon Music	Orchestra
40.	"SWING" (Continue, orchestra only, as link to next scene.)	DEMON and FAIRY

SCENE 3.

41.	"LOVERS"	PRINCE and PRINCESS
42.	Ace music, reprise 6	Orchestra
43.	Demon music, reprise 39	"
44.	"SALUTE THE QUEEN"	CHORUS and RUMMY
45.	Reprise 44 for march off	Orchestra
46.	Glass rising, reprise 11	"
47.	Glass descending, reprise 12	"
48.	Ace music, reprise 6	"
49.	"SOMETHING STIRRED"	Ensemble
50.	Mood music	Orchestra
51.	Fairy music, reprise 38	"
52.	" " " " (Continue as link to next scene.)	"

SCENE 4.

53.	Ace music, reprise 6	Orchestra
54.	Sorcerers' music, reprise 27	"
55.	Demon music, reprise 39	"
56.	Glass descending, reprise 11	"
57.	Glass descending, reprise 12	"
58.	"WHAT'S EVIL?" (Continue, orchestra only, as link to next scene.)	ACE, DEMON and JACK

SCENE 5.

59.	Ballet	FAIRY, QUEEN and CHORUS

60.	Entr'acte.	

PART 11

SCENE 6.

61.	"GIRLS"	PENNY and CHORUS
62.	Ace music, reprise 6	Orchestra
63.	Reprise 44, slowly for march in	"
64.	Fanfare, reprise 26	"
65.	" " "	"
66.	" " "	
67.	"LOVE STORY"	PRINCESS, KING, QUEEN and PRINCE
68.	Ace music, reprise 6	Orchestra
69.	Glass rising, reprise 11	"
70.	Glass descending, reprise 12	"
71.	Scene finale (Continue, orchestra only, as link to next scene.)	QUEEN and CHORUS

SCENE 7.

76.	"THE SORCERERS' SONG"	SORCERERS
77.	Glass rising, reprise 11	Orchestra
78.	Glass descending, reprise 12	"
79.	Ace music, reprise 6	"
80.	Fairy music, reprise 38	"
81.	" " " " (Continue as link to next scene.)	"

SCENE 9.

82.	"DOGGEREL DITTY", song sheet	QUEEN and AUDIENCE
83.	Fairy music, reprise 38	Orchestra
84.	Whooshy music, link to next scene	"

SCENE 10.

85.	Monster's entrance music	Orchestra
86.	"MONSTER'S SONG"	MONSTER
87.	Glass rising, reprise 11	Orchestra
88.	Glass descending, reprise 12	"
89.	Fairy music, reprise 38 very fast	"
90.	Chase music	"
91.	Fight music	"
92.	"THE QUEEN OF HEARTS" (Continue, orchestra only, as link to next scene.)	Ensemble

SCENE 11.

93.	"SWING", reprise 40	FAIRY and DEMON

SCENE 12.

94.	"IT'S SUMMER", reprise 2 for walk-down	Orchestra
95.	Fanfare, reprise 26	"
96.	Glass rising, reprise 11	"
97.	Glass descending, reprise 12	"
98.	"IT'S SUMMER", finale, reprise 2	Tutti.

EFFECTS PLOT

PART 1

SCENE 1.

1.	Police siren	Off L.
2.	Loud explosion	Maroon
3.	Pistol shots	Off L.

SCENE 2.

4.	Noise of powerful car approaching, ending in crash	Grams. or tape.

SCENE 3.

5.	Car approaching	Grams. or tape.
6.	Car door slam	Off L.
7.	Car backing out, plunging forward and receding into distance.	Grams. or tape.
8.	Loud explosion	Maroon
9.	Loud explosion	Maroon

SCENE 4.

10.	Car approaching, screech of brakes, door slam.	Grams. or tape.

PART 11

SCENE 8.

11.	Loud explosion	Maroon
12.	Roar of jet motors	Grams. or tape.
13.	" " "	" "
14.	" " "	" "
15.	Loud explosion	Maroon
16.	Roar of jet motors	Grams. or tape.
17.	Car approaching, screech of brakes	" "
18.	Loud clonk	In flies

SCENE 9.

   19. Outboard motor   Grams. or tape.

SCENE 10.

   20. Loud crash   Off as convenient

   21. Outboard motor   Grams. or tape.

   22. Backfiring, (pistol shots)   Off R.

   23. Burst of noise from outboard motor   Grams. or tape

   24. Loud explosion   Maroon

   25. Car approaching, screech of brakes and a bonk   Grams. or tape.

   26. Car roaring off into distance   "   "

www.ingramcontent.com/pod-product-compliance
Ingram Content Group UK Ltd.
Pitfield, Milton Keynes, MK11 3LW, UK
UKHW021843210426
5322IPUK00022B/438